GRANDAD'S JOURNEY: A HOLOCAUST MYSTERY

By Bernard S. Wilson

MP
Marigolde Publishing

Grandad's Journey : A Holocaust Mystery by Bernard S. Wilson

Marigolde Publishing

Editors: Lucas J. Golding and Janis Hunt Johnson/www.askjanis.com
Book Design: Jeff Altemus, Align Visual Arts

ISBN: 979-8-9859004-0-8

To Jules Wilson Tixier and all the children
who must know and not forget...

PREFACE

Bernard S. Wilson wrote *Grandad's Journey: A Holocaust Mystery* at the request of his grandchildren, who wanted to know more about the French region on the Mediterranean where they spent many vacations together. Bernard had accidentally discovered that the beach towns where they liked to spend their summers had been the stage for atrocities during the Spanish Civil War and World War Two. He too, wanted to know more about it!

Bernard had another good reason for writing his novel: he had been contacted by a man, Dr. Ronald Friend, Professor Emeritus at Stony Brook University in New York, who had been interned in a French camp as a child and who, unlike his father, had been saved from deportation to Auschwitz. But Dr. Friend didn't know who the person was who had rescued him, although he had reason to believe that his rescuer was somehow linked to the Quakers' office in Toulouse, France. Ron asked Bernard to help him find that person, as Bernard had by then done a substantial amount of research on the Quakers and the aid they provided war refugees. The story that emerged from Bernard and Ron's investigation was not only fascinating, but it also unraveled information about the camps that might have remained untold to young—and not so young—readers.

Dr. Friend explains in his own words: "I am the person who as a two-year old was rescued by Mary Elmes, and who is the inspiration for Bernard Wilson *Grandad's Journey*. In this novel," he adds "Bernard Wilson vividly illuminates without loss of accuracy the dreadful situation and predicament that Spanish and Jewish families, like my own, found themselves in during World War Two. The story of Mary Elmes' heroism in saving Jewish children from certain death is portrayed thrillingly in the form of a mystery."

In Ron's opinion, "It should be of interest to all who wish to learn more about Hitler's genocidal policies in Vichy France, and those like Mary Elmes who exhibited such bravery."

Dr. Rose Duroux, Professor of Hispanic Studies at the *Université Clermont Auvergne*, was one of the children who crossed the Pyrenees from Spain into France in 1939 to escape Franco's regime. The welcome given the Spaniards was far from what they expected. The living conditions were atrocious. And she, too, feels she owes a lot to the Quakers! Rose became very close to Mary Elmes in the ninety-nineties until Mary's death in 2002. She also shared many memorable conversations with Mary's colleague and 'accomplice', Alice Resch Synnestvedt. Both played a large role in the rescue of children of the Spanish Civil War and World War Two.

"*Grandad's Journey*," Rose explains, "is the suspenseful investigation of a nearly eighty-year old mystery. The narrative weaves together two catastrophes of the 20th century, the Shoah and the *Retirada*, through the very real itinerary of Mary Elmes, Irish heroine awarded by Yad Vashem. Before saving dozens of Jewish children from the camps, she risked her life during the Spanish Civil War. From 1937 onwards, she treated children along the "road of death" between Málaga and Almería and then followed them from one Quaker hospital to the next to the Rivesaltes camp, where another tragedy awaited her, as this camp soon became the appalling purveyor of lives to Auschwitz. Intertwining fiction with historical facts, the author reconstructs the rescue of two Jewish children."

"Refugees" and "internment" are unfortunately not terms relegated to the past, but are still very present today. Bernard Wilson reminds us of this with a committed and engaging novel that will be read in one sitting.

Marianne Seidler Golding, Professor, Southern Oregon University

CHAPTER ONE
Emma's Homework

Cobh, Ireland, March 2019

Martin White glanced at the clock on the classroom wall. He had just about enough time to introduce the last homework assignment to be done over Spring Break.

"Option number three," he said. "Those of you who aren't interested in number one or two may find this one more to your liking. I'm challenging you to learn about your own family's history! History isn't just about dates, kings, taoiseachs[1], and so on. It's about you as well, and people like you."

He was on his feet now, walking around the classroom as he explained the homework: "This challenge — this assignment— is to learn about your ancestors, who they were and what they did. Where they lived, where they came from, how many children they had, what sort of life they had. Once you've done this, you'll be able to see where

---

[1] The Irish word *taoiseach* means "chief" or "leader"; thus the Taoiseach is the Prime Minister and head of the government of Ireland.

you fit into the history of our little corner of the world."

He paused at a desk near the front of the room. "You haven't chosen a topic yet, Emma, have you? Does this appeal to you?"

"I've never really thought about it," she admitted. Emma Collins, like the other students in the class, was just sixteen years old, and more interested in the present than the past. But she did enjoy the history lessons that Mr. White taught. He was younger than most of the other teachers in the school, not much older than Emma was herself, she thought. Perhaps that was why she never found his lessons boring or tedious. He had a way of making every lesson seem fresh and lively. It was never just a list of facts to be remembered, but always something that made her think, and challenged her opinions.

"How many of you have watched the show *Who Do You Think You Are?*[2] He was addressing the whole class now. A few hands went up. "How did you like the stories? Were they interesting? Yes, John?"

John Braddock, a tall boy sitting at the back of the room answered, "They're okay, but they're all about celebrities. They're not about ordinary people like us, so I can't really relate to their stories." This was met with a collective groan from the rest of the class, as John had a reputation for being annoying.

"Well, here's your chance," Mr. White responded. "Discover the stories at the root of *your* family tree."

After the class ended a few moments later, Emma approached the teacher's desk and asked, "How do I get started on the family history project?"

"The first thing you should do is talk to a relative, maybe a

---

[2] *Who do you think you are?* is a genealogy documentary series in which celebrities trace their family tree with the help of historians.

grandparent. You need to be able to go back to 1911. Your great-grandparents would have been alive then. Your grandparents will be able to tell you their names, where they lived, and when they were born. Are any of your grandparents still around?"

"Yes, my grandfather is alive and well. And he only lives about a mile away, so that's no problem. But what do I do with this information?"

"That's where the year 1911 comes in! Every ten years, with years ending in a one, there was a national census. They were kept secret for a hundred years, so the earliest census we can access is from 1911. If you have an extra five minutes, I can show you what to do."

As she walked home, Emma thought about the assignment. It sounded interesting, maybe even fun. And it was useful too because she would end up knowing more about her own family, what sort of people they were and what kind of problems they'd had to face. Perhaps she would find out where her artistic skills came from. She was quite good at art, whereas when her mother and father tried to draw, nobody had any idea what the drawing was supposed to be. It made playing Pictionary very stressful; nobody wanted to be on Dad's team!

She tried to imagine what her family's lives would have been like back in 1911. Where did they live? Were they well-off or poor workers in factories? Or perhaps farm-hands working every hour and living in cottages without water or electricity? Suddenly, Emma found herself filled with a burning curiosity; she couldn't wait to get started. And that meant going to see Grandpa! Tomorrow was Saturday. She would go and see him then.

Emma's family ate dinner at 6:00, when her father got home from his office job in the center of Cork. Her mother worked in the nursery school nearby so she had plenty of time to get home and prepare the meal. However, on the weekends, her father insisted on doing the cooking, and Emma and her older brother Andrew would often help out as well.

Today her mind was not on food, because she was already planning how she was going to approach Grandpa about his family. She was tempted to discuss her plan with her parents during the meal, but something held her back. She thought she would keep the whole thing to herself until she had made some progress. It would just be her and Grandpa. For as long as she could remember, her grandfather had been an important part of her life. When she was little, she enjoyed the times she had stayed at her grandparents' house with its enormous garden out in the country and its wonderful view of the Cork harbor. But that had been when Grandma was alive. Now poor old Grandpa lived by himself, and he had moved to a small apartment just twenty minutes away to be closer.

"You're quiet tonight, Emma," said Dad. He was watching her as she mindlessly pushed her shepherd's pie around the plate. "Something on your mind?"

She smiled. "Yes," she said, "but it's a secret — well sort of, for now, anyway. Something I need to talk to Grandad about. I think I'll bike over tomorrow to see him."

"We ought to have him over for a meal this weekend," Mum said, looking up. "It's been some time. Why don't you invite him here for Sunday? Give him a call. Then you won't need to go over there tomorrow. You can just talk to him here."

Emma shook her head. "No, I will ask him of course, but I want to talk to him alone first. I need his help on something I'm doing at school. I'll tell you all about it after."

"Okay," said Dad. "But don't bother him with anything too complicated, will you? Remember, he's not as young as he used to be, and he's not been the same since your granny died."

Emma arrived at her grandfather's apartment around 11:00 on Saturday morning. Alan Collins, her grandfather, was looking out for her through his window on the second floor. He always enjoyed her visits, although they were not as frequent as they used to be. He reckoned that she was busy with school and homework, and whatever other activities teenagers did these days. He was glad that she was busy, not hanging around with friends, smoking, and getting up to trouble like other kids her age. He was well into his seventies now, and finding life rather difficult without Doreen, his wife who had died after a battle with cancer some five years before. But his son's family members were always there when he needed them, and sometimes even when he didn't. Like now, for example. He had planned to do a couple of hours of gardening this morning in the little garden patch allocated to his place, but that would have to wait if Miss Emma needed him.

He opened the door and gave her a hug. "Lovely to see you, Emma. Come on in." The kettle was on, and soon after there were two cups of tea on a little table in the corner. Emma would have preferred a diet coke, but she knew she wouldn't be getting one here.

After the customary small talk ("How's your mum? How's it going at school?") Emma brought the conversation around to the reason for the visit.

"I'm glad you mentioned school, because that's actually what I wanted to see you about. I need some help with the history project I'm thinking of doing."

11

The old man raised his eyebrows. "History was never my strong point. I doubt if I can help you much there."

"Well, as a matter of fact, you're the *only* one who can. If you can't, then the project is off! You see, it's the history of our family. I need to trace our family — your family — back as far as I can."

Alan looked at his granddaughter with an expression of surprise. This was obviously not what he was expecting. After a moment's silence he said, "If you want my advice, you should do your project about your mother's family."

"No, it's got to be the Collinses," replied Emma. "My teacher said it's much easier to follow the male line, because you don't have to deal with name changes every time someone gets married."

12

Grandad got up and walked over to the window. With his back to her, he looked out at the fields across the narrow lane. Then he turned and faced her. "Darling," he said, "you know I'm always glad to help you when I can, but this time you've asked me for something that I just don't think I can do. Like I said, try your mother's family. I'm sure your Granny Alice would be delighted to get all her albums out and tell you all about her wealthy relatives!"

"It doesn't matter whether your parents were rich or poor, Grandad! My history teacher says that by the time we've traced back to the beginning of Queen Victoria's reign, we are bound to have found relatives to be proud of as well some who let the family down. That's the point of this project. To see what kind of a mix we are. Did you know that if I go back about seven generations, that would mean about sixty-four different ancestors? And that's just on your side of the family!"

Alan Collins came and sat down across from her. "Darling, I can't help you! You see, I don't know who my parents were. I never knew them. I was adopted when I was very young. It's not something I talk about, because it's not a big deal to me. To me, Mum and Dad were the people who raised me. If there was anyone before them, I never knew them. And I don't want to know now. So, please accept that there's nothing I can tell you."

Emma felt a stab of guilt as she remembered how her father had warned her not to bother him. Yet she was so astonished to hear this that she couldn't help asking, "Does Dad know that you were adopted?"

"Yes, of course. And your Uncle Ben, too. I told them when they were about your age, and it didn't bother them. In those days nobody knew much about the time before their parents, and certainly not about the time before their grandparents. There was no Inter-whatever to look up these things like you can do now. And I might never have known to this day if it weren't for that football tournament."

Emma was puzzled. "What football tournament?"

Grandad smiled ruefully. "I was twenty-two. I had been playing for the town club for a year or two. We had invited a team from France to come over. It was one of these friendly things. I don't know how they got here. I don't think there was a ferry service then like there is now. I guess they had to fly. Anyway we were invited back — somewhere near Roscoff, I think it was. And I needed an identity card or a passport. Not many people had such things in those days. I'd never been abroad. Nobody my age had. Well, to get a passport, I needed my birth certificate, so I asked my mum if she knew where it was. She burst into tears! She said that she had been dreading the day when she'd have to tell me that she wasn't my real mother."

"So what happened?"

13

"Well, there wasn't a birth certificate — at least not anything that could pass as one. I had to use the adoption papers. And the whole process took so long that I ended up missing the trip to France after all. My poor old parents had to tell me they weren't really my parents at all, and it turned out to be all for nothing!"

Emma tried to wrap her head around this unexpected development. "So you have no idea who your birth parents were? Didn't the adoption papers tell you anything?"

The old man shook his head. "They showed that I was about three at the time of adoption, and that I had been in some kind of institution before that. That was all."

"Didn't you want to know?"

"As I've said — it was a long time ago, and things were different then. It was at the end of World War Two. I suppose I was what they called a 'war baby,' perhaps the child of some poor girl not much older than you, and the father probably a soldier from America or Canada or somewhere else. Even if I could have found my mother, there would have been no hope of finding who my father was. And you say that it's my father — the biological one — that you need to know about?"

"If I'm going to trace the Collins family, yes! Because it's the…."

She went silent for a moment, and then, looking up at her grandfather, her eyes wide with concern, she said, "But I'm not even a Collins, am I? You're not a Collins either. Neither is Dad! I can't believe it! Who am I? What's our real name?"

Her grandfather got up and put his arm around her. "You go into the kitchen and find us some cookies. I'm going into the spare bedroom for a minute. As for who you are — you're Emma, my lovely granddaughter, and what your real surname is or might have been doesn't matter one bit."

With that, he walked out of the room and down the hallway.

A few minutes later, as Emma was putting some cookies on a couple of plates, she heard a noise from another room which sounded like something being dragged across the floor. Just as she was about to go see if her grandfather was doing okay, she heard his footsteps coming back towards her. He came into the kitchen carrying a shoebox tied shut with string. Setting it down on the kitchen table, he undid the string and took out a big manila envelope.

"These are some photographs that my father took when they first got me. That's me, that little chap, and that's my mum holding me in her arms."

15

Emma took the picture and examined it. "Your mum, well not your *birth* mum, but the one who raised you — she looks quite old to have a small child."

"She would have been in her forties, I think. But Dad, he was much older. Probably in his mid-fifties. Here he is, look."

He passed Emma another picture. It showed an elderly looking man sitting in a garden chair wearing a knotted handkerchief on his head. "He wasn't a fit man. He was in the British Army in World War One and he was lucky to have survived. He had been in the trenches and seen some terrible things, which he never really got over. But I'm afraid this is not my biological father."

Emma picked up a picture that had fallen out of the envelope. She turned it over and examined it. On one side there was a faded image of two people in front of a house, but part of the picture was missing as if it had been torn off. On the other side there was some indistinct writing which she couldn't make out.

"What's this, Grandad? What's this a picture of?"

He took it from her, adjusted his glasses and inspected it closely. "I remember this one," he said. "I remember putting it in the box with those photographs years ago. It was something I found when I cleared the house out after my mother died — quite a while before you were born. I have no idea what the picture is. I don't recognize the place or the people. It had some foreign-looking words on the back of it as I remember, but I can't make them out now."

There is writing on the back, there," Emma said, pointing at some shapes that looked like letters, "but it's too faint to make it out. Can I take it home and show Dad?"

"Well, let's take a better look at it first." With that, Alan opened a drawer and took out a large magnifying glass. After a minute of squinting through the glass, he passed it to his granddaughter. "It's no use," he said. "It's impossible to make any sense of this. I don't even know why I bothered to keep it. I've never been able to fathom it out."

But Emma had other ideas. "Let me take it home," she pleaded. "Maybe Andrew will think of something."

The old man sighed. "All right, then. Now let's have our tea, and you can tell me more about how things are going at school."

CHAPTER TWO
The Code

Philip and Helen Collins were not pleased with their daughter. She had upset her grandfather by asking personal questions and forcing him to tell her that he was adopted. This had always been a family secret, and Philip Collins saw no reason why his children should ever need to know about it. So after a severe telling off, Emma went to bed without mentioning to her parents the torn photograph and unreadable message.

The next day grandfather arrived for lunch, but not a word was spoken about what had happened the day before. Emma didn't think it would be a good idea to show the picture with the mysterious writing to her parents after what they'd said the previous evening, and her brother Andrew was away camping with some friends. So she had to be patient and wait until the weekend was over.

The following Monday at school, she told her history teacher about her situation and explained that it was unlikely she would be able to do the family history project. He was sympathetic and suggested that she maybe trace her mother's family instead. However, Emma was a bit stubborn, and not quite ready or willing to give up just yet. She still had the picture in her bag, and she was determined to solve this puzzle.

During the afternoon break, she finally got a chance to show the picture to her brother. "Grandad doesn't recognize the place or the people," she said. "But what do you make of the writing on the back?"

He held it up to the light, but it was no use. "What if we tried image enhancement with a computer?" he asked.

"What — you mean like the police do? With blurry CCTV videos?"

"Yes! Something like that. We could try putting it into Photoshop, and then mess around with different settings to see if we could make something stand out more clearly."

"Okay! Let's try that. Let's meet in the IT lab after school."

One hour later, and after getting permission to use the scanner, they were looking at an image of the strange writing on the computer screen. It was still illegible. But as Andrew moved the sliders to alter the brightness and contrast, it became almost possible to make out the shapes of some letters.

"I think we can make a guess at this," he said at last. "Some of these letters are quite clear now, but there are others where we'll just have to use trial and error until something makes sense."

"But it's not in English, is it?" objected his sister.

"Just write down the letters as I read them out. Then we'll try to make some sense of it. The first two letters are still really difficult —

18

my guess would be an *f* and a *p* but I can't be sure. Then there's an *i*, a *c* and a *k* — no doubt about those. Then it looks like it could be a *p* again, followed by *a*, *u*, *c*, and *h*." Perhaps it would be a good idea to underline the letters that I'm just guessing."

A few minutes later they were both looking at what they had come up with. Emma had written:

F P I C K P A U C H P I V F S A L T F S I L O T K

"There are some English words there," said Andrew. "Look, there's *pick*, *salt* and there's *silo*. And *Auch* isn't English, but it's a town in France, I think. And so is *Pau*!

"But it doesn't mean anything," objected Emma. "And of course, we can't be sure about those six letters I've underlined. Do you think it's in code?" 19

But Andrew wasn't listening. He had just seen Mr. White pass down the hallway, and was up on his feet and after the history teacher as fast as he could go. A minute later they were both in the room, looking at the screen.

Emma showed Mr. White the mysterious photograph and explained how they had managed to decipher most of its contents. "Have you any idea what it could mean?"

"Well, let's have a look at this picture first. It's quite old I should think, probably around 100 years or so. Look at the style of clothing these people are wearing; I don't think it's Irish, either. That's not an Irish house. It's most likely Eastern Europe, I'd say. Very interesting! Many people were beginning to afford small 'box' cameras in those days. The photographs were in black-and-white of course, and didn't come close to the quality our pictures have today. Now, let's see what this writing says."

He examined the writing, and then looked again at what his students had written down. "Tell me more about this photograph. Where did you get it?"

So Emma told him about the big manila envelope with the ancient photographs belonging to their grandfather, and how this picture with the writing on the back had been hidden in the envelope for years. Again, she asked, "Can you understand it? What does it mean?"

Mr. White drew up a chair and sat down at the computer desk. "There's one word there that stands out for me. It's not spelled quite right, but you had to guess some letters, didn't you? If those *f*s are really *e*'s, and the *p* is an *r*, then you've got the word *Rivesaltes*."

20

"And what does that mean?" asked Andrew.

"Don't you know? Haven't you come across that word recently? Think hard!"

Emma and her brother stared at each other. A look of realization brightened Andrew's eyes.

"Holocaust Memorial Day! It was something we heard about then. But I can't remember exactly what. It has something to do with 'the Irish Oskar Schindler,' doesn't it? Somebody from Cork, I believe?"

Now it was Emma's turn. "Oh yes, it was a lady called Mary something wasn't it? I can't remember her last name, and I still can't see where *Rivesaltes* fits into it!"

"Okay—let's put your grandfather on hold for a bit. You need to remind yourselves about Mary Elmes first — that was her name — and what she did in the Rivesaltes internment camp. You have had a lesson on all of this, and it's been in the papers and on TV, so you should know all about her — especially as she came from Cork — just down the road from here! I want you, Emma, to prepare a short talk about Mary Elmes and present it to the history class when we come back after Spring Break. Do you think you can manage that?"

Emma was hesitant. "Where am I going to find the information?" she asked.

"Oh, come on, Emma! Where do all you young people get information from nowadays? Just Google her name, for a start. And there are two books in the library, both by journalists up in Dublin: Clodagh Finn and Paddy Butler. But you probably won't have time to read those all the way through. You should be able to get enough from online sources for your presentation, and you can fill in more details next term. I only expect about twenty minutes or so. Just enough to remind everyone what we're talking about. Unless I'm very much mistaken, this is all going to be relevant to your Grandad's story, too!"

So once she got home, Emma rather reluctantly put the strange photograph with its mysterious writing away safely in her bedroom; and having borrowed the two books mentioned by her teacher, she did some reading about Mary Elmes, the woman they once called "*The* Irish Oskar Schindler."

The first that Irish people had heard about this remarkable woman was in an article in *The Irish Times* in January 2012. It was another five years until two books were published in 2017 telling the story of her life. Since then Emma had been taught about her life and work several times at school; on Holocaust Memorial Day, and in her history class with Mr. White. So she already knew some basic

21

facts — that Mary Elmes was born in Cork, that she had worked in Spain and France with children affected by the wars, and that she had recently been awarded the title of "Righteous Among the Nations" — the first and only Irish person to receive this honor. But if she had to fill twenty minutes of a history class presenting about her, Emma would need to do some serious research.

CHAPTER THREE
Mary Elmes

It was Tuesday, April 30th, the day when Emma was scheduled to give her presentation about Mary Elmes. She had done quite a lot of research at home over the break, using both the books she had borrowed from the school library and some articles she found on the Internet. There was certainly no shortage of them, although many contained the same information she had already learned. She had her notes carefully prepared, and she was confident that she knew what she was going to say and how she was going to say it. But she still felt nervous; it was the first time she had ever been asked to speak in public, other than just being called on to answer a question or two in class.

"Good morning, everyone," said Mr. White. "I hope you all had a good Spring Break and that you're ready to get down to some serious business this term. This morning we're starting off by reminding ourselves about Mary Elmes, the first Irish person to be honored by Yad Vashem as 'Righteous Among the Nations.' But before I hand it over to Emma to present what she has found out about Mary Elmes,

I think that I should explain to you all what *Yad Vashem* is and what those words mean.

"*Yad Vashem*," Mr. White continued, "also known as The World Holocaust Remembrance Center, was opened in Jerusalem in 1953. It is a vast museum and center for historical research, and its first objective is to record the names of all those who died in the Holocaust. Survivors of Auschwitz and the other death camps realized that the six million victims who had been murdered were only known by the numbers tattooed on their arms. They wanted these people to be identified and known by their names. *Yad Vashem* is Hebrew for 'a name and a place' — a place where these people could be properly remembered. Nearly five million people's names are recorded there, but there are still over a million names that have yet to be recovered. And there's another list of names there too: people who were not Jewish, but risked their lives to save Jews. So far, there are 27,362 people known as Righteous Among the Nations — and just one of them is Irish. That person is, of course, Mary Elmes. And so, now over to you, Emma."

Emma stood up and walked to the front of the classroom. "So that's what makes Mary so special, that she's the only one — so far at least. Since Ireland was a neutral country during World War Two, there wasn't much opportunity for brave Irish people to rescue Jews from the Holocaust. Mary was the exception. She was already in France when the war started. She was able to take over the work that British people had started.

"But her story began several years before that, when, after doing really well at school in Cork and up in Dublin, she went to Spain to help in the children's hospitals, which were opening during the Spanish Civil War."

"Was she a nurse, then?" someone asked from the back of the room.

"No, she wasn't. That's why getting into Spain wasn't easy, I'm not even sure how she managed it. But she was taken in by a group of British women, mostly nurses, who recognized how useful her ability to speak Spanish was. She had to keep moving as the fighting progressed across the country, and she was responsible for finding empty buildings that could be turned into hospitals to care for injured and sick children. There are some lovely stories of children she was able to help. She didn't keep a diary but she did take photographs, and they were kept in a book with brief notes about each child."

John Braddock had his hand up. "How did she get so good at speaking Spanish?" he asked.

"Well, I told you that she did really well at school in Dublin, but I didn't bother you with all the details. She studied at Trinity College, where she won a gold medal, and got a first-class degree in French and Spanish. She had stayed in both Paris and Madrid to perfect these languages, so she was an ideal person to run the hospitals in Spain, and later to work in France. Now, where was I?"

"Lovely stories about children," someone called out.

"Yes, that's right," said Emma, looking at her notes to find her place. "Children whom she had helped made her drawings and paintings. There was one boy called Pepe who was very sick, but he managed to make her a New Year's card which she kept for the rest of her life. Her family still has it. It meant so much to her because poor Pepe died a few days later."

"I think that we'd better move on to her work in France now," Mr. White said, looking at his watch.

"Well, in 1939 the war in Spain came to an end, and thousands of refugees poured over the mountains between Spain and France. It was a bitterly cold winter, there was snow and ice everywhere and the journey was treacherous, especially with the German planes attacking them."

"Why German planes? What had Germany got to do with it?" asked a girl sitting by the window.

As Emma hesitated, Mr. White stepped in.

"We need to talk about the Spanish Civil War another day. Germany sent planes and warships to aid the Nationalists.[3] Some people say that it was Hitler's rehearsal for the Second World War. It's all a bit complicated, but you are right to ask. Let's stick with Mary Elmes for now. Emma?" He gave her a nod.

"Well, all these people ended up on the beach in France. That sounds good, but it wasn't. There was no shelter, and the refugees were closed in by barbed wire on one side and the sea on the other. Mary had returned to Cork, but she soon volunteered to come to France and to help these poor people. She was able to buy things like books, art materials, musical instruments and toys for the children to make their lives more bearable. This is when people started to call her 'Miss Mary.' She had time for everyone, she listened to their problems, and she promised to do everything she could to help them. And she did help a lot to improve their living conditions."

John Braddock had his hand up again.

"You said it was 1939. Wasn't France at war with Germany then?"

Emma glanced at Mr. White hoping that he would step in again.

---

[3] The Spanish Nationalists were led by General Franco during the Spanish Civil war against the Loyalists faction who supported the elected Republican government from 1936 to 1939.

"It was February when the refugees arrived in France," explained Mr. White. "The war with Germany didn't begin until September. But when it did, it brought thousands more refugees from Belgium and Holland as well as from the north of France, all wanting to put a safe distance between themselves and Germany. Then in June 1940, France fell and the country was divided. The northern half and the Atlantic coast were occupied by Germany, while the southern half was ruled by a French hero of the First World War. He was Philippe Petain. Unfortunately, he took his orders from Germany, and it was under his rule that the persecution of the Jews began in France.

"Now Emma, tell us what Mary Elmes did to help these Jewish people."

"Well," Emma began, "all the Jews in the south of France were put in a terrible internment camp called Rivesaltes. I'm especially interested in this, because I think that my grandfather might have been among them. Mary visited this camp nearly every day, and soon she was as well-known there as she had been on the beaches. Many of the people in this camp were the same Spanish people who had been on the beaches themselves. They were moved into Rivesaltes before the Jews arrived later. There was no heating in the blocks where they lived, and there were no water or toilets indoors; they had to go outside for those things. Soon, there were rats and lice everywhere, and diseases began to cause deaths, particularly among the children and the old people.

"Mary got permission to take children from the camp to empty houses and hotels — by the sea or in the mountains — where the children could enjoy good food, keep warm in the winter, wash themselves properly and wear clean clothes. They had to return after a month or two so that others could take their place. But when the trains came to take the Jews away to some unknown location, Mary realized that she must at least try to save the children."

Emma held up two large books. "You will have to read these books or articles on the Internet to find out exactly how she did this. It is believed that she saved several hundred children from certain death.

"But it wasn't just Jewish children that Mary helped," Emma continued. "There was a terrible shortage of basic food items at that time. Children were coming to school without any breakfast, and there wasn't anything to eat at home for dinner, either. So, Mary arranged for food to be imported and paid for by America, and then she distributed it to the children in the schools. She asked the teachers to weigh the children every week, and she kept a record of every child in every school over a wide area so that she could see if they were gaining weight as they should.

"She probably saved even more lives of French children than she did of the children in the camps. Eventually, the Germans occupied all of France, and soon after that they came for Mary. She was arrested and ended up in a Gestapo prison near Paris. She was held there for six months. How she was treated, nobody knows, because she never spoke about her time in prison. After the war ended, she married a Frenchman and had two children. She lived to be 92. By the time she died, she and her work were completely forgotten."

Another boy had his hand up.

"How is it that we only just found out about her?" asked Connor.

Mr. White stepped in again. "Mary never wrote anything about her work. She didn't even tell her two children about it. It wasn't until someone in America whom she had saved started to ask questions about how he had escaped the Holocaust that the whole story gradually emerged. As Emma says, there's a lot more to this story in the books she has been reading, and you should all try to find time to read them yourselves. Was there something else that you were going to say, Emma?"

"Yes. I had found out that nearly all the time Mary was working in Spain and in France, she was working with a group of people called Quakers. In Spain it was mostly British Quakers, but in France it was the American Quakers. I didn't really know anything about Quakers, but I found out that they are a religious group of people who always seem to pop up when there is an emergency of some kind. In fact, I found out that after the war ended in 1945, and everything gradually got back to normal, the first Nobel Peace Prize after the war was awarded to the British and American Quakers in 1947. So, I reckon we can say that Mary Elmes played a part in winning a Nobel Prize!"

Mr. White was astonished. "I didn't know that, Emma," he said. "Well done in finding that out. That's fantastic! That's a real achievement for you, as I'm sure that's not a well-known fact at all.

"Well, everybody, Emma has given us all an excellent start to the term, and we will all be eager to see if she can find out the truth about her grandad. So, many thanks, Emma, and very well done! Everybody — let's show our appreciation!" The whole class rose and applauded as Emma blushed.

CHAPTER FOUR
The Camp

Philip Collins was not in a good mood. He had just gotten home from work and opened the one letter the postman had delivered that was addressed to him. It was from their travel agent. It seemed that the hotel on the Greek island of Santorini, which he had booked for the family holiday in August, had suddenly closed. It was all due to some financial crisis in the Eurozone, and in Greece in particular. Apparently, the family would not lose the money he had paid as a deposit, but he would have to find someplace else — quickly!

Emma had been thinking hard about everything she had learned while researching the life of Mary Elmes, and she realized that her history teacher may have been onto something about the mysterious torn-up picture. Her grandfather may have, at some point, been in the Rivesaltes camp, and he could well be Jewish. So, when Emma got home, anxious to discuss the matter with her family, her father was not in a particularly receptive mood.

"I wish you'd leave this business alone" he snapped. "I've told you that Grandad doesn't want to be bothered with all this digging into his past. Anyway, we've got enough problems to worry about right now. We've just lost our holiday in the sun!"

That brought Emma back to earth with a jolt. She had been looking forward to their vacation in Greece. They had been there the year before last, and the dream of long lazy days on the beach in Santorini had kept her going during winter term. Now it wasn't going to happen! It was a gloomy dinner that evening, and as soon as it was over she went up to her room and turned on her computer. Maybe she could distract herself from the disappointment by finding out more about Rivesaltes. There was certainly plenty of information online. There were even pictures, showing old, rundown huts surrounded by weeds and rubbish, and in the distance, what looked like a wind-farm, similar to the one she had once seen out to sea off the coastline somewhere. It seemed that the remains of the camp were still there, after all these years! But how could she be sure that her grandfather had really been there himself? Perhaps even born there? Why would an Irish child be in a French concentration camp? What would the family make of that? What would Grandad say if it were true?

Emma found a Website devoted to the Rivesaltes Memorial Museum. There were some amazing pictures, and she clicked on them to read more details. But it was all in French! On the site there was a little British flag, and clicking on it brought up a page in English. But it was only a page of information about access, opening times, and admission prices. The important pages with pictures were only in French! Frustrated and tired, Emma gave up, and when she finally went to bed, she couldn't get the camp out of her mind. At least the disappointment of the cancelled holiday was completely forgotten.

A couple of miles away, John Braddock was looking at his computer screen. Emma had shown him the mysterious photograph, and he remembered that it had other letters on it, too. After the name of the camp, he had noticed what looked like the French word *îlot* followed by the letter *k*. As soon as his computer was fired up, he typed *îlot k* into Google. There were, as usual, many Websites to choose from. But there, just four or five items down, he read "Rivesaltes, France, *îlot K*, the children's section of the camp."

He clicked on it; it led to a picture of a boy with a bicycle inside some kind of hut. There were other pictures, too, and all of them were of children. As he clicked through the photographs on the Website, John began to form a picture of this place called Rivesaltes. It was big, flat, and dirty; and this part was full of children. Where were their parents? The caption said that îlot K was the children's section of the camp. So were their parents somewhere else? He remembered that Emma had said that the children were kept together with their parents until the age of fourteen.

33

The next day, Emma sought out the history teacher as soon as she could.

"Where exactly was Rivesaltes?" she asked.

"Let's see if we can find it." He pointed to the map of Europe on the wall. "We'll start with Perpignan, the nearest big town. Do you know where the Pyrenees are?"

Emma pointed to the border between France and Spain. "Down here, aren't they?"

"Right! Now, go up the coast a little way. What do you find?"

"Got it!" Emma turned to her teacher with a smile. "Here's Perpignan — not far from Spain, and almost on the sea. What sort of place is it?"

"Very nice!" answered Mr. White. "I've spent several holidays in that region with my family. I prefer the mountains myself, but there are some lovely beaches there."

Emma was still looking at the map, tracing the coastline with her finger.

"But where's this Rivesaltes place? Where the camp was?"

"It won't be marked on that map; it's too small. But it's very close to Perpignan. Just a bit the other way — away from Spain, I mean."

His student looked thoughtful. "So — do you feel certain that my Grandad was there? Would there be some sort of register we could look at?"

"There could be — possibly in the Perpignan archives. But I'm not sure if there would be a complete record of all the inmates. They were coming and going all the time. But you told me that your grandfather was an orphan. If he was in this camp, it's almost certain that at least one of his parents would have been there, too." He paused, turned away, and looked out the window. "Emma, you already know that that place was a sort of assembly center for all the Jews in the south of France. Thousands of them were sent from there to the camps in Poland."

"Like Auschwitz, you mean? Are you saying that my Grandad's parents were sent to Auschwitz?" She swallowed hard. "Why wasn't he sent, too?"

"That's what we've got to find out. But you've already discovered that many children were rescued and hidden away. He could have been one of them. He was too young to remember, of course. We need a name, and then we could be certain. I don't suppose your

34

grandfather knew his biological parents' names?"

"No — he didn't even know his parents weren't his actual parents, until he was grown up. All he has is that picture."

Her teacher thought for a moment. "Are you sure there's nothing else? Nothing else written on the picture, I mean? Have you got it with you?"

"No, but I've got what I wrote down when we fiddled around with it in Photoshop." She opened her bag and brought out the sheet of paper. "There are a few letters before the word *Rivesaltes*. It looks like *f p i c k p a u c h*."

Mr. White looked at the paper. "But you've underlined the *f* and the two *p*'s. Didn't you say that they were very indistinct? What if we change the *f* to an *e* and the *p*'s to *r*'s, like we did before? Then, look! We get *E r i c k R a u c h*. That's a name, surely? It could be *Erick Rauch* or *Eric Krauch*. Either way, it sounds very German to me."

Emma shook her head. "It's all getting a bit beyond me," she said. "You're saying, then, that my grandfather is German, and Jewish, and that his parents were killed in Auschwitz? That's terrible —how can I tell Grandad that?"

Her teacher smiled. "Hang on, hang on! At the moment this is just a theory. It's the way it looks. But you don't know for sure that that piece of paper even has anything to do with your Grandad. It could be sheer chance that it got mixed up with those photos you told me about. But from my point of view, as your teacher, this is all good stuff. It's teaching you to check your sources. That's what learning history is all about. You see, if you were a tabloid newspaper editor, you'd be rushing out the latest edition with the headline, 'Local sixteen-year-old girl's family perished in the gas chambers.' But that's not history. That's sensationalism."

"So, what am I going to tell my family?"

"I think you've got to tell them that there's a possibility — even a very strong probability — that your grandfather may have been rescued from a French concentration camp... and that you need their permission to go on researching. If they — your dad or Grandad — say *no*, then that's it. Job done. Leave it there."

"And if they say *yes?*"

"Well, then we'll have to research the name *Rauch* or *Krauch*."

"Can we do that?"

36

"As l said before, there may or may not be registers of the inmates of that camp still in existence. But there are lists of all known victims of the Holocaust. We could start there."

CHAPTER FIVE
An Embarrassing Encounter

On her way home from school, Emma heard footsteps behind her.
When she turned around, she saw John Braddock hurrying to catch
up to her.

"This is a bit out of your way, isn't it?" she said curiously.

John was embarrassed. When he saw her leave for home he impulsively
followed her but hadn't had time to think of what to say. So, for lack
of any better conversation starter, he quickly began to tell her what
he had discovered last night about *ilot k*.

"It seems that it refers to a special area in the camp reserved for
children," he explained.

"So it's some sort of address, I suppose? You know that there were
other things written on that photograph, too, don't you? Well, me
and Mr. White have worked out that it was someone's name —
probably a German."

John resisted the temptation to correct Emma by telling her that she should say *Mr. White and I*. He was particular about his speech. But he felt that this wasn't the time or the place.

"What was the name?"

"We're not certain, but it could have been *Erick Rauch* or *Eric Krauch*. You remember those letters at the beginning of the line?" She showed him the photograph again.

"Well, there you are then. You've got a name and an address. What are you going to do now?"

"I don't know. My Dad doesn't want me to bother my Grandad anymore. He's really cross with me for starting all this."

38 "Well, I think that you've got every right to know who your ancestors were. You never know if you might need to know something about the medical history of your grandparents. People get asked that sort of thing when they are taken ill, or even just when they are filling out forms for insurance."

"Yes, I never thought of that. You've got a good point there. I'll have to tell my mum and dad, I suppose. And then, if they agree, I'll also tell Grandad."

There was a toot of a horn, and looking up, Emma saw her mother's car pull up. The window opened.

"Jump in! I got away a bit early today!" Then, realizing that there was a boy with her daughter, she added, "Does your friend want a lift, too?"

Emma was embarrassed. She wanted to say *No, he's not my friend,* or even *No, he's not with me*; but that seemed a bit rude. So she just mumbled, "He doesn't go our way!" She got in the open door without even saying good-bye.

"Who was that then?" asked her mother. "You were a bit short with him."

"Well, I didn't ask him to follow me! He's just someone from my class at school."

"Did he want something from you?"

"No — he was just...." She didn't know what to say. This wasn't the time to start telling her mother about the camp. "I'll tell you later."

Mrs. Collins glanced at her daughter and wondered what was going on. So far, Emma hadn't seemed to have been particularly interested in boys, but she supposed it would have to start sooner or later.

Emma was furious with John for being there at that moment and causing her such embarrassment. She began to regret that she had allowed him to become involved in her family's affairs. It wasn't as if she even liked him. The rest of the short journey home continued in silence.

Emma helped her mother prepare dinner, and neither spoke of the incident again. When Dad came home, the atmosphere changed, and it was clear that he was in a much better mood.

"How do you two fancy a camping holiday?" he asked, putting down a bunch of leaflets on the table, even though his wife was trying to set it for dinner.

"In a tent?" she asked anxiously. "I don't fancy that!"

"Not the sort of tent you have in mind," he replied. "Take a look at this!" He opened up one of the leaflets that showed what appeared to be the interior of a very luxurious tent indeed. It was titled *Paradise in Provence, Aquitaine, or the Languedoc.*

"It's our best bet after losing the hotel in Greece. We don't have time to be choosy. It's France!" he explained. "I fancy Provence myself. Good climate — the next best thing to Greece."

Emma put down the plates she had pulled from the oven where they had been warming up and looked at the brochure. On a map of France, there were three stars marking the three locations of the tented villages. They were all down near the south of France — one on the left, one on the right, and one in the middle.

Her father pointed to the star on the right. "We could go to this one in the region of Provence, here. It's just outside of Nice. We need to book quickly if you fancy it."

Emma looked at the star in the middle. It looked as if it could be near where she knew Rivesaltes to be. "What about this one?" she asked.

"Argelès-sur-Mer," her father read. "In the Languedoc, whatever that is! Why do you ask?"

"Well, it's about Grandad." And she told her parents all about the concentration camp, and how it might — just might — be the answer to the mystery of who her grandfather really was.

That night Mr. and Mrs. Collins were lying in bed discussing the day's events.

"I'd no idea that she was doing all this digging around in Dad's affairs," complained Emma's father.

"It's not just her! It's that Mr. White, the history teacher. And that boy she's got mixed up with as well," said his wife.

"And Andrew, too, apparently," said Mr. Collins. And then, as his wife's words had just sunk in, he asked, "What boy she's mixed up with?"

"Some lad in her class. She says that there's nothing in it. But you don't know what to believe, do you?"

"Oh well, she's sixteen now, you know... But this is a real mess! We're going to have to tell her Grandad the whole story. I just hope he doesn't get too upset."

41

But in fact, when Emma's Grandad was told the following evening what she had been up to, he was surprisingly calm about it. Andrew had gone to an orienteering course with some friends, Emma was at home, and their parents had driven over to Grandad's apartment to break the news to him.

Philip Collins thought it best if the children were not there when his father was told about the concentration camp.

"I thought you would be furious!" said Mr. Collins. "You always told me that it was something you didn't want discussed."

"Yes, but as it turns out, there was no reason for me to worry. You see, I didn't want some unsuspecting family to find out that their grandmother had had an illegitimate child all those years ago. And that perhaps this child, now grown up, would be knocking on the door demanding money in exchange for keeping quiet about it. I realize now that it was kind of silly of me!"

"But aren't you upset by the thought that your parents might have died in one of the death camps? If it's true, that is."

"Of course — of course that's dreadful. I don't think I want to know those details. Let them rest in peace, whoever they were. But I would like to know who I owe my life to. And who you owe your life to, come to that. And Emma. And Andrew."

Mrs. Collins spoke up. "So you wouldn't mind if the children found out the circumstances of your escape?"

"This is crazy," interjected her husband. "We're just going along with this story as if it's proved beyond all doubt. There's probably nothing in it at all."

"Let Emma see what she can find out," said his father. "And why don't you go on vacation at that place you mentioned? The campsite is near where I might have been born. There's no harm in that."

CHAPTER SIX
A Breakthrough

John Braddock walked home slowly after the awkward encounter with Emma's mother. He felt embarrassed about it, and realized that Emma was embarrassed, too. If they had both been boys (or both girls, for that matter) it all would have been perfectly normal. Why did people have to be so silly about boys talking to girls? Couldn't he be friendly and helpful to Emma without feeling guilty if he was caught talking to her? To be honest, he thought, he didn't really know whether it was the buzz he got from successful research that was pulling him towards Emma, or the fact that she was a girl (and a rather attractive one at that). He decided that he would push on with the challenge of finding out about her Grandad on his own, and avoid any further incidents like the one that had left him blushing furiously.

So that same evening he sat down at his computer and resumed his research. First, he tried Googling *Rivesaltes*. This brought up loads of information which he had already seen, but didn't give any clues as to how he would look up the name of a particular prisoner in the camp.

Then, after several more unsuccessful searches, he typed in *people who rescued Jewish children from Rivesaltes.* Within a few minutes he discovered that there was a French organization called OSE[4] that had been responsible for doing just that, and that they still existed! They even had a page on Facebook.

Now John was not a fan of Facebook – or Snapchat or Twitter, for that matter. He couldn't understand why his classmates would want to spend time writing to each other every few minutes about which store they had just been in, or what they thought of something they had just seen on TV. Fortunately, he discovered that he didn't need to join Facebook in order to contact the people at OSE. There was a button which said *Contactez-nous,* and John's French was more than sufficient for him to know that this was the way to go. He thought about trying to send his request in French, but decided against it. He wrote:

44

> *Dear OSE,*
>
> *I am trying to find the person who was responsible for saving someone called Erick Rauch or Eric Krauch from the Rivesaltes concentration camp during the War. Can you help me, please?*
>
> *Yours sincerely,*
>
> *John Braddock*

That night he did not sleep well. He worried about whether or not he had done right by meddling in Emma's research, and if the French organization he had emailed would be able to help them. He also wished fervently that he had not had that encounter with Emma's mother.

---

[4] OSE : Œuvre de secours aux enfants (Children's Aid Society), is a Jewish humanitarian organization that helped Jewish children in France during and after World War Two.

The next morning, John was waiting for Emma at the school gates. She saw him there, and tried to avoid him, but it was no use. He approached her with a big smile. All memory of yesterday's embarrassment was apparently gone as he thrust a piece of paper at her and said, "Read this!"

Emma took the paper reluctantly and started to read. It was an email, and it said:

Dear M. Braddock,

Thank you for your inquiry. We have searched our records and we are sorry to inform you that we have found no references to children with the exact names you mention. However, there are several children with the surname Rauch, but with different first names. There is also a Franz Krauch, born February 13th 1942, removed from the camp at Rivesaltes on September 13th 1942. He was rescued by a representative of the American Friends Service Committee[5] and taken to their colony at Vernet-les-Bains.

We hope that this information will be useful to you.

Yours sincerely,

Hélène Dubois

Œuvre de Secours aux Enfants

"Is that any help?" asked John.

Emma read the message a second time and gasped. "That's Grandad's birthday," she said, "February 13th. He was seventy-seven this year. So, yes — it would be 1942."

45

---

[5] The AFSC, created in 1917, is also known as the American Quakers. This organization helped civilian victims of several wars.

"So do you think that's him? How does he know his birthday if he was adopted?

"I don't know, it's just something we've always known. As to whether it's him or not, it does look like it. But it's still not proof, is it? I mean, it could be a coincidence. And if his name was Franz, who was Eric? That was the name on Grandad's photograph."

John shrugged. "His brother perhaps, or his father?"

Emma was in a bit of a daze from all this information. Suddenly she snapped out of it. "Where did you get all this from? What have you been up to? And what's this — this foreign group, these people who've sent the email?"

John could see that things were going to get difficult. "Let's ask Mr. White, and see what he thinks. After school?"

Emma agreed reluctantly. "Okay, after school."

Andrew Collins had returned from his orienteering course later that day, so it was the three of them who made their way to the history classroom at 3:30 that afternoon. Emma had sent a text to Andrew asking him to meet her there, but he was surprised to see John Braddock turn up as well.

"What are you doing here?" he asked — rather rudely Emma thought, though she realized she had been rude herself earlier.

"I've been able to find out a bit more about your Grandad," John explained, handing him the email.

"I don't understand," complained Andrew. "What's all this about?"

"There's been an awful lot happening since you left," said Emma. She proceeded to bring her brother up to date with what had transpired. "John's been doing some research himself, and may have come up with Grandad's real name, and the name of his rescuer's organization."

It was at this moment that Mr. White arrived, and Emma filled him in on the latest developments.

Mr. White was impressed. "I think that's pretty smart of John to get this far," he said. "This could be a useful lead. But it's got to be backed up. What we need is some documentary evidence that links the name of Franz Krauch to that of Eric Krauch. Any ideas?"

The three students looked at each other helplessly.

One by one they shook their heads.

47

"Okay! Then I think this is a job for me. We've obviously got to contact this American group. It's a Quaker organization. I can look up their details and send an email asking for help. I think it'll come better from a teacher. Leave it to me. It's only morning time there at the moment. If I email them when I get home, I could get an answer tonight."

CHAPTER SEVEN
Not Odd, Just Different

When Dad came home that evening, he announced that he had found the perfect campsite for the family.

"It's in that place that you picked out the other day," he said to his daughter while pulling a brochure from his pocket. Argelès-sur-Mer. Listen! This is what it says: '*Camping Sud* is in a wonderful location just meters away from a stretch of uncrowded, sandy beach. There are splendid facilities offered, including pools, a spa, and great entertainment. This is a great choice if you are traveling with teenagers — in peak season there is a nightly disco just for them.' How does that sound?"

Andrew said it sounded great, but Emma wanted to know if it was near Grandad's camp.

Mother rolled her eyes. "Can't you think of anything else at the moment? We're planning a holiday, not an archaeological expedition."

"It's not archaeology — it's history," Emma responded. "And anyway, it's not just any old history — it's *our* history."

"Well, it may be yours, but it's not mine!" said her mother.

"I hadn't thought of that," said Andrew. "That's weird, isn't it? But hey, are we all Jews, then?"

"Good God," cried Dad. "We must be! I never thought I'd say that...."

"No, we're not," replied Emma. "I asked Mr. White that yesterday. Apparently, you're only Jewish if your mother was. Grandad might be — we don't know yet. But you're not, Dad, and nor are we."

Dad shook his head in disbelief. "I can't get my head around this! But anyway, from what you say it's all unproven yet. Let's get back to this campsite. Do we go for it, or not?"

There was general agreement that they should try to book a family tent in *Camping Sud* for one week, beginning on the first Saturday in August. After that, they would drive up the coast to another campsite near Nice and spend two weeks in Provence.

An hour later it was all done and settled.

The following morning Emma was back in the History classroom to see Mr. White again. He looked up and smiled as she entered the room. "I'm sorry, I haven't heard anything yet. Come and see me later." Then, just as his pupil was turning to go, he added, "By the way, that was a great bit of detective work that your friend John Braddock did for you yesterday. I'd never heard of that French organization, and without the information that he got from them, you would have been really stuck."

"You mean about Franz Krauch?"

"Yes. I think there's little doubt that he's your Grandad — but of course we've still got to make sure. Yes, you owe John a great deal. I hope you thanked him!"

"Yes — yes, of course," she replied with a little uncertainty. In her head she was thinking, *Well, no, I didn't really. Perhaps I'd better ask him along later, too.*

So later that day, John and Emma were back to see Mr. White. But this time he seemed rather less confident that they were heading for success.

"I got a reply to my email," he said. "The archivist at the AFSC headquarters (that's the American Quakers, by the way) said that they have a huge volume of files relating to the Rivesaltes camp. There are mentions of individual children — quite a lot, in fact — but they are not indexed, so he can't just give us a simple answer to our question. He says that he doesn't have the necessary means to undertake a search of the files himself, as it would be an enormous task. However, he says that we are welcome to search the files ourselves."

"Does he mean online?" asked John.

"No, apparently not. They have been digitized, but not uploaded to the Internet."

"So that's it, then," said Emma. "We're no further forward. Unless I can persuade my dad to take us all to America!"

"Well, there is just one other possibility. A copy of the digitized files has been placed in the United States Holocaust Memorial Museum."

"Where's that?" asked John.

"In Washington, DC, in America."

"So we *will* have to go to America!" cried Emma.

Her teacher laughed. "There's another copy. In France."

"At the Rivesaltes camp?" asked Emma.

Mr. White smiled. "No, not even that far away. It's in the *Mémorial de la Shoah* in Paris. That's the Paris Museum of the Holocaust. *Shoah* is the Hebrew word for the Holocaust, and many countries including France use that word. Is there any possibility that your family could take you there?"

52

"Well, we are going to go to the south of France in August, so I suppose we could maybe stop in Paris on the way down."

"Excellent," said Mr. White. "If I were you, I'd email them to say you're coming, and explain what you want to find out. You will probably have to do the searching yourself once they've set you up, so count on being there for a whole day — even two!"

Emma and John went down the stairs together.

"Well, that's it then," said John. "Good luck with the research in Paris. I'm sorry I won't be able to help you."

"You've been a great help so far. I'm sorry if I haven't seemed very grateful."

"That's okay. You probably think I'm a bit pushy, getting involved in your business. Actually, it's not like me at all really. I didn't find it easy speaking to you about it but I couldn't help it, I was so interested in what you were trying to do."

Emma didn't know what to say. She couldn't really say, *Yes, you were a bit out of order.* So she just smiled and thanked him again. They walked on together and out the door.

As they approached the gate, where their paths would go separate ways, John said, "I've really enjoyed helping you. And not just because I like the challenge of a mystery. It was good to work together with someone." He paused. "I do most things on my own," he added.

Emma was about to walk off down the road, but she stopped and turned back. "Yes, you do seem to be by yourself most of the time," she said. "Don't you feel lonely sometimes?"

53

"All the time," he said bitterly. "You don't know what it's like being an only child. Everybody thinks you're spoiled, a mama's boy, that sort of thing. I've heard people talking about me. I didn't ask to be an only child. It wasn't my fault my parents couldn't have any more children."

"But there must be a lot of advantages, too," said Emma, wanting to put an end to this conversation but not knowing how to do it. "I mean, you don't have to share everything like me and Andrew do!"

Like Andrew and I do, thought John, but he just said, "You know those things you want to know about, but you can't ask your parents?"

Emma nodded.

"Well, if you have brothers and sisters, you can talk to them about those things. Us only-children have no one to ask!"

"Hmm — I suppose! Anyway, I've got to head home. So — thanks again. Bye!"

"Bye, Emma. See you tomorrow!" And John was gone.

Emma walked home deep in thought. If she'd thought about John Braddock at all, it was as someone who was a bit odd, a bit different. Someone who found schoolwork easy, and who preferred not to get involved in the fun and comradeship of the others. Everybody knew there were boys — and girls — like that. They were just different, a bit weird, some of them. It had never occurred to her that they might have wanted to be more friendly but didn't know how to do it. She resolved to try to be a little less quick to make judgements about people in the future.

CHAPTER EIGHT
Chaos in France: A History Lesson

Emma and Andrew felt that they needed some more help from their History teacher. It certainly seemed likely that their grandfather really had been saved from the Rivesaltes camp, but how had he gotten there in the first place?

So, during the lunch break they found Mr. White and asked him if he could help them some more. They told him that they would probably be able to go to the Museum in Paris, but they needed some advice on what to ask when they got there. First of all, they wanted to know how it could have come about that their grandfather was in the Rivesaltes camp—with or without his family.

"It seems so strange that a baby should be in prison—and without his parents," said Emma.

"Oh, I think we can be sure that he was with his mother. It was only the older children who were separated from their parents. And, of course, fathers and mothers were separated from each other, too. The older boys would have been with their fathers."

Emma nodded. "Yes, I found that out when I was doing research on Mary Elmes."

"As to how he came to be there — well, his name suggests that his family was Jewish and from Germany. When Hitler came to power in 1933, it soon became obvious that things were going to get difficult for the Jews, so the wise ones who could afford it got out — to France, Belgium, Britain, America — any country that would have them. Then, when France and Britain declared war on Germany in 1939, your grandfather's family, now in France, would have been arrested and placed in hastily thrown-up camps, mostly in the countryside. They did the same thing in Britain with any German families, just in case there were spies among them. When the authorities were satisfied that they didn't present any threat, most of the women and children were released, and many of the menfolk, too. This was during the period they called 'the phony war'[6]. Now — you tell me, Emma — what happened in May 1940?"

"The fall of France?" she asked with a little uncertainty.

"Not yet! That came a month later. But during that month thousands and thousands of people from Belgium and Holland poured into France, and together with the people of northern France, this great tide of humanity choked the roads leading to the south. Your grandfather's family would have been among them. But by the middle of June, it was all over. France had fallen. The northern part was occupied by German forces, but the south became the 'non-occupied zone,' controlled by a new French government based in the spa town of Vichy."

"But my Grandad wasn't born until 1942!"

---

[6] The phony war refers to the eight-month period, from October 1939 to May 1940, when almost no fighting took place on the Western front.

"That's right. It would have been just his mother and father. They would have lost everything except what they had been able to carry with them. They would have had to queue up at feeding stations along with all the other refugees. And they would have been friendless because they were Germans."

"But they would have been free to manage as best they could, wouldn't they?" asked Andrew.

"Not for long! The new French government in Vichy needed to blame the sudden defeat on someone, so they started to imitate Germany — and put the blame on the Jews. It wasn't long before laws were passed, similar to those in Germany, which had made your grandfather's family leave home in the first place. Those who were teachers, doctors, lawyers — all the professional classes — found themselves out of work. They had to register as Jews, and their identity cards were stamped with a *J*, which made it impossible for them to find other employment."

"And they had to wear a yellow star on their clothing, didn't they?" asked Andrew.

"Well, actually, no! That was about the only thing that the Vichy government didn't copy from the Germans. That was only made compulsory in the north — the occupied zone. But your grandfather's family would have found life becoming more and more difficult. They probably would have tried to keep a very low profile. The best solution would have been to move on again, but no one could leave France without an exit visa. And to get one of those you had to apply at the town hall, which meant exposing yourself to more trouble."

"So how do you think they ended up in Rivesaltes?" asked Emma.

"Well, in 1942, the Vichy French police started rounding up all the

Jewish families and placing them in camps. Eventually, they moved them all to this one huge camp near the Spanish border, and then via Paris to the extermination camps in Poland. Rivesaltes became a sort of waiting room before the final journey."

Emma shuddered. "But surely people must have known what was going on. Didn't anybody try to stop this from happening?"

"Yes, there were those who spoke out against packing people up like animals into trucks and sending them off to an unknown fate. The Archbishop of Toulouse, for one. He ordered an address to be read from every pulpit in the diocese condemning what was happening. But to be honest, there was little anyone could do. It was too late. Except for one thing — and that was to try to save the children."

"How did they manage to do that?" asked Andrew.

"For some time, various relief agencies like the Red Cross had been taking children out of the camps and sheltering them in old mansions and castles, with the approval of the authorities. It relieved them of the responsibility of feeding and clothing them. They were supposed to go back to the camps eventually. But when the time came for the trains to be filled with Jews, Gypsies, and other so-called 'undesirables,' the relief agencies managed to hide many of these children away, ensuring that the trains left without them."

"But their mothers and their fathers went on the trains?" said Emma.

"I'm afraid so. And that's how so many children ended up as orphans, just like your grandfather."

Emma sighed. "I don't know if I really want to see this camp, when such terrible things happened there. But I do want to try to find out who this person was who rescued Grandad. I suppose they will be dead by now, but it would be good to find their children if they had any."

"And that'll take some detective work," said her teacher. "Good luck!"

That evening, Emma told her family about the latest developments in her search for the truth about Grandad.

"You're really sure that it was Grandad who was there in that camp, aren't you?" said her father.

"Yes, I am! Everything seems to fit! But I can't wait to get to that museum in Paris. Mr. White thinks we might get the proof we need there."

Dad sighed. "So that's something else that needs fixing. We need to find somewhere to stay near Paris on the way down. I'll see to that tomorrow."

CHAPTER NINE
The Holocaust Museum

The Collinses emerged from the Paris *Métro* at the *Hôtel de Ville* station and found themselves in a drizzle on the busy main road. Dad had his Paris guide in his hand and was trying to work out which way was north.

"If the sun were shining, I'd know which way to go!" he exclaimed. "But I don't know which side of the road we're on, so I don't know whether to go left or right."

"Is it far from here?" asked Emma's mother.

"Just a couple of streets along, then further down towards the river."

"I think this is the *Rue de Rivoli*," said Andrew helpfully.

"I know that! But which side of the road are we on?"

"Let's walk along a bit and see the names of the streets on this side of the road. Then you can check them in your guide, and we'll know whether we're going the right way or not!"

Mr. Collins considered that Andrew's orienteering course was perhaps not a waste of time after all. It seemed like good sense, though he didn't say so. He found it a bit difficult to be put right by one of his children.

Emma was saying nothing. She had noticed that several of her friends had posted comments in their WhatsApp group chat about her recent interactions with John Braddock. They were completely over the top, of course. He was just being helpful, that was all. She found herself defending him in her mind when she saw that he was being referred to as a *nerd* or a *creep*. She wondered what he would make of it. He probably didn't use WhatsApp, but someone would surely enjoy telling him what was going on. Anyway, the whole situation had upset her, and she didn't feel like sharing it with the rest of the family, either.

"Yes, this is right!" said Dad. "We are going the right way. We need to turn down here and it should be on the left."

It soon became obvious that they were in the right place. There were a number of children milling around, probably it was a school party, thought Emma. She wondered where they had come from. They seemed to be reading names on a wall. Then she remembered Mr. White telling her about the wall of the "Righteous Among the Nations" — men and women who had risked and sometimes lost their lives to help Jewish families. She wondered if Mary Elmes, the lady who had rescued so many Jewish children, would have her name on that wall.

The entrance to the Museum was through a complicated system of doors and a metal detector like the ones they had passed through at airports. Mrs. Collins was astonished at the security and asked what could possibly be so important as to require this level of protection.

"That's not it," said Dad. "It's the threat of terrorists that they're concerned about. This is a Jewish museum, so this place is a sitting target."

It was rather uneasily that the family entered the museum, partly as a result of the tight security and partly because of their limited French. They didn't know how they were going to achieve what they had come for. They were about to follow all the other visitors when Emma spotted a desk with a sign bearing the word *Recherche*.

"I think we need to go there," she said.

The woman behind the desk looked up, smiled, and said something in French. Emma looked helplessly at Andrew, who was pretending to examine a poster on the far wall.

"Are you English?" asked the woman, in perfect English.

"No," replied Emma. "We're Irish. But we speak English, of course."

"I'm sorry," said the woman. I thought you were English because your father spoke to you in English just now. We don't get many Irish visitors here! Now, how can I help you?"

Emma explained the purpose of their visit, and the woman — whose badge indicated that her name was Monique — showed them upstairs to one of the research rooms.

"There are a few formalities you will need to deal with first," she said, "and you will need to leave your belongings in the lockers around the corner there. My colleague Sabine will explain everything to you. I hope that you will find what you are looking for." With that, she was gone.

After they had stowed everything away in the lockers except for the pencils and notebooks they were allowed to keep, Sabine showed them to two computers. Andrew and Emma sat at one, and their parents at the other. The assistant gave each pair a stack of papers, many pages stapled together.

"This is a guide to the collection. It's not an index, but it will show you what is in each folder. The collection is divided into eighty-four boxes, each box contains several folders, and each folder has many pages in it. Do you know which office you are interested in?"

64

The Collinses looked at each other, unsure of what that meant. Sabine saw their confusion, and asked if they knew what camp the person they were trying to find had been in.

"Oh yes," replied Emma. "It was Rivesaltes!"

"In that case, you will need to search the files of the Perpignan office. They are in boxes one to twenty. You will look for name lists, and letters referring to prisoners. Many of the folders are just concerned with supplies and other routine matters — you don't need to bother with them. The Rivesaltes camp was closed in November 1942 , so you won't need to look at anything dated later than that."

She smiled at them as they stood there looking overwhelmed. "It may seem like looking for a needle in a haystack at first, but you'll soon get used to it. Do you understand French?"

---

[7] From November 1942 to 1944, the camp was used to house German troops. Later on, more "undesirables" were interned on and off at Rivesaltes until 1977 (see Chapter Eighteen).

Again, they looked at each other, wondering who would answer first.

Andrew spoke up. "I'm probably the best, but I'm not very good. Will all the records be in French then?"

"Not all of them, but probably many of them are. If you need any help, don't hesitate to come to my desk and ask." With another smile, she walked away and left them staring at their screens.

"This is a blow," said Dad. "I didn't think that we were going to have to read French. Maybe it would be best if we swapped places. You sit with me, Emma, and Andrew, you help your mother."

It must have been two hours later when Andrew shouted, "Hey! Look at this! I think we've found it!"

Several other researchers in the room looked up in surprise and Andrew muttered an embarrassed "Sorry," followed by "Er — *pardon!*" as soon as he realized where he was.

The family gathered around the screen. They read:

> *To: Mary Elmes*
>
> *From: Joan Groves*
>
> *Date: September 10th, 1942*
>
> *Dear Mary,*
>
> *We have just received the following cable from our London office, and will appreciate any news you can report to us in regard to this case:*

SPECIAL URGENT REQUEST YOUR HELP THROUGH PERPIGNAN OFFICE ASSISTANCE CASE 57 ERIC KRAUCH AND FAMILY ÎLOT K BARAQUE 35 RIVESALTES STOP

This is the case we wrote to you about on September 7th. We wonder whether the whole family is still in Rivesaltes, or whether they have been deported already. Can you investigate for us and let us know as soon as possible? Thanks so much for your trouble in this matter.

Sincerely yours,

Joan Groves

"Wow!" cried Andrew. "This is it!"

"But it doesn't give the names of the family members," objected Dad. "We still can't be entirely sure it's my father's family."

"Try moving on," said Emma. "These letters are often answered a few pages later. I've noticed that several times."

Andrew scrolled down the screen. Each page was in English, which made the search much easier than they had feared.

"What's this?" said Dad. They read:

To: Joan Groves

From: Mary Elmes

Date: 12th September 1942

Dear Joan,

In reply to your letter of September 10th, we know the case of Eric Krauch and his family quite well. The father has been sent away temporarily to some labor camp in the north.

The mother and the children are all still at Rivesaltes. The two children will probably be liberated this evening from the camp of Rivesaltes and we are sending them to Vernet-les-Bains.

There was a lot more about another family, but Emma was not reading any further.

"This must be right," she said. "But I don't understand — it says 'two children.' Who's the other one?"

"Perhaps it was a child from another family," suggested Mother.

"No — it definitely says 'the two children.' Grandad must have had a brother or a sister," Andrew insisted.

"Well, in that case, why didn't that French organization that John found mention that there was another child?" asked Emma. She fished in her bag and produced the email John had given her. "Here it is, look! It just says, *He was rescued by a representative of the AFSC.* Surely they would have mentioned it, if there were two of them."

"And we still don't know for sure that Grandad was even one of them," said Andrew. "Though the dates add up, and the fact that they were being sent to that Vernet-les-Bains place can't be a coincidence."

Dad stood up and stretched. "We're getting tired! We've done enough for today. We've still got tomorrow. Let's pack up for now and find something to eat!"

Mother said, "I know just where to look. It's somewhere in that main road called the BHV — the *Bazar de l'Hôtel de Ville*. There's bound to be a restaurant there."

"What sort of place is it then?" asked Andrew.

"It's a big department store. I was reading about it in a magazine the other day."

Andrew looked at his father and rolled his eyes.

"Come on then, lead the way!"

That night, Emma couldn't sleep. Images from the pages she had read flashed through her mind. She kept trying to picture what life must have been like for the families back then in the camp. It was some time before she fell asleep, and even then, in her dreams she continued the search for her grandfather's family.

CHAPTER TEN
Perpignan, France

Sunday, September 13th, 1942　　　　　

The office of the American Quakers was actually the ground and first-floor rooms of a private house on the Avenue des Baléares in Perpignan. It was a handsome house on a handsome street of three-story buildings, in one long continuous terrace, but each one individually styled. Number 30 had balconies on the first and upper floors.

Mary Elmes, the delegate in charge, lived in her apartment on the top floor. It was well-furnished with a modern kitchen and bathroom, and her sitting room overlooked the street below. There were trees in the road that reached up almost to the level of her apartment and afforded welcome shade from the summer heat. Her bedroom at the back of the house overlooked a small shady garden and was well away from any street noise. Not that there was much street noise, for this was the second year of strict rationing, and motor vehicles were scarce. Gasoline was in such short supply that some buses were powered by gasogene, the fumes from a wood burner towed behind the vehicle.

Mary was an Irish woman who had overseen children's hospitals in Spain during the Spanish Civil War. She had arrived in Perpignan with thousands of other refugees who had struggled over the Pyrenees in February 1939 to escape General Franco's pursuing armies. If she had been Spanish instead of Irish, she would have been in one of the several camps surrounding Perpignan, living in appalling conditions. But thanks to her nationality, she was in pleasant and comfortable surroundings — though like everyone else in wartime France, she was subject to all kinds of shortages, including food.

It was late afternoon on a warm sunny day, and Mary had just finished dictating a batch of letters to Jeanne, her secretary. Jeanne was French, unlike most of her staff who were Spanish. Mary had rescued them from the camps and so had saved them from the monotony and drudgery of life there. Her task had originally been to work with these unfortunate people — mostly women and children — to ease their lives by setting up classes for the children and providing materials such as books and musical instruments for the adults. Now her work involved other camps, where Gypsies, Jews, and other so-called "undesirables" were being concentrated — in even harsher conditions, if that were possible.

"Will you call Victor and tell him that I'm ready to go to Rivesaltes now?" she asked her secretary.

Jeanne   lifted the telephone and called the chauffeur who, as well as driving Mary to the various camps, acted as a mechanic and looked after the two trucks used to deliver supplies around the district.

"He says that there will only be just enough gas," she said, putting the phone down.

Mary smiled grimly. "He always says that, yet somehow we manage! I'll have a chat with the Prefecture tomorrow and see whether they will provide more coupons for us."

"Are you bringing any children back with you this time?" asked her secretary.

"Yes! The two Krauch children. There's another convoy due to leave tomorrow and I'm determined that they will not be on it. Isobel wrote to Marseilles this morning saying that I would ensure their release tonight. There's nothing we can do for the mother I'm afraid. You know, I sometimes feel as though we are just making it easier for the government to send these unfortunate folk away by looking after the children for them. If the Germans ever occupy this zone, the children will be taken, too. We shall have to sneak them all out before that happens."[8]

Jeanne sighed. "I don't know how you manage to persuade parents like Frau Krauch to give up their children," she declared. "I know I would never have let mine go if I had been in Argelès."

"But your children would not have been in danger of being sent to their death," retorted Mary. "Your children have the good fortune not to be Jewish."

71

"Do you really believe that these people are taken away and killed?" asked her secretary doubtfully. "The word is that they are being resettled in Silesia to work in the mines."

Mary snorted in disbelief. "Children? Babies in arms? Old women on crutches? Patients dragged out of their hospital beds? I don't know where they take them, but they never come back! Some of the fit men like Herr Krauch are sent to work camps, and usually they come back after six months or so. But when those trains leave Rivesaltes, they are never heard from again. And why just the Jews? Never the Spaniards — thank God. But why not? If they are supposed to be a work force, you'd expect them to be drawn from the fittest of all races and religions."

---

[8] It was in fact France's President and Secretary General of the Vichy regime's police force who insisted that the Jewish children be deported to the death camps.

"They do send Spanish people," protested Jeanne. "What about old Señorita Garcia? She was Spanish!"

Mary shook her head sadly. "Yes, she was Spanish. A Spanish Jew."

The door opened and a weather-beaten, elderly man appeared. "The car is ready, Madame!"

"Thank you, Victor. I'll only be a minute. I'll see you outside."

Captain Humbert picked up the ringing telephone. He listened for a moment and then hung up without a word.

He stood up, reached for his cap and strode to the door just as the old Citroën pulled up alongside the building. The window of the vehicle was lowered, and the arm of Mary Elmes emerged. The captain shook her hand.

"Good afternoon, Madame Elmes! Where do you wish to go today?"

He knew full well of course that the Quaker representative could have only one reason for seeking permission to enter the camp of Rivesaltes this Sunday afternoon. Tomorrow, the fifth convoy was due to leave for a so-called "unknown destination." It was his task to see that everything was ready for its departure, and that the required number of inmates was loaded onto the train when it departed at 7:00 in the morning.

They had already been selected and warned to be ready. There were nearly 600 men, women, and children this time, ranging in ages from four to eighty-three, in the case of an old man. Of these, 450 of them, all Jews, had only arrived on Friday from the camp of Les Milles near Marseille. The other 150 or so had been waiting a little longer and had been rounded up from various places in the unoccupied zone. No doubt Madame Elmes would be seeking to remove some more children from the camp. Well, provided they were not among the twelve under-sixteens already selected, he had no objections. He respected the tall Irish Quaker with her brisk no-nonsense manner, and he felt that she understood him, too.

Mary Elmes smiled at the captain. "To îlot K, as usual," she replied. "I have found some space for two more children, and I would like your permission to remove them from your care."

Mary knew that the captain disliked his job, and that he cooperated with the various caring agencies to the utmost of his abilities. That was why she opposed some of the other agencies in their desire to withdraw from working in the camp. They felt that by cooperating with the authorities, they were also implying that the conditions in Rivesaltes were satisfactory — and of course they were not. The inmates were ill-fed and ill-housed. They lived in squalor with rats running everywhere, and the only clothes they possessed were the clothes they wore when they entered the camp. Yet to withdraw their services would mean that the caring agencies were turning their backs on these poor people as a matter of principle.

73

"There should be no problem," replied the captain. "There will be the usual formalities of course, I will need to see the parents' permission in writing, and as usual I will need to know where the children are to be placed. They must be available to be recalled to the camp at any time should Vichy so demand." He knew, and Mary knew, that should this ever happen, the children would be found to have mysteriously disappeared from their registered colony. Such things had happened before.

The Citroën made its way through the dust and dirt to the entrance to îlot K. Like the camp itself, îlot K was also surrounded by barbed wire, and the only access was through another guarded gateway. The passes were shown and checked, and Mary got out of the car to make her way to barrack number thirty-five. As it was a warm day, most of the women were sitting outside the barrack on improvised seats — upturned boxes and crates. There was no recognizable furniture in the barracks at Rivesaltes.

She found Frau Krauch sitting on her own with her baby in her arms. Her little girl, Lotte, nearly three years old, was playing nearby with some other children.

"Hello, Helga!" said Mary.

Helga Krauch lifted her head, and Mary saw that she had been crying. She touched her on the shoulder and said, "I've come to take your children, my dear! You know that you can trust me with them. They'll be well looked after and we will get them away to safety as soon as possible."

Helga held the baby out towards Mary and said, "Take him. Take my little Franz. He's too young to know what's happening to him. But I'm not letting Lotte go!"

The Quaker worker was appalled. "But Helga, only yesterday you agreed to let them both go. You signed the papers. I have them here. And Captain Humbert has given his permission. You can't turn down an opportunity like this."

The Jewish mother was crying again. "I don't know what's to become of us all, but I could never face my husband again if I had to tell him that I let Lotte be taken away. I owe it to him to see that no harm comes to her. What sort of mother would I be to let a child who has had three years of my love be taken from me? Who is going to explain to her why her mother doesn't want her anymore?"

Mary Elmes was silent. What could she say? Could she tell this woman what she suspected lay in wait for her at the other end of the railway tracks? And supposing she was wrong? Supposing there was a new life awaiting them all with proper accommodation and good food? Children and parents were dying here in this camp from malnutrition and disease. Could anything be worse than this?

"Is that your final decision?" she asked.

The young woman nodded. She pulled from her pocket an old photograph of the family home in a village near Breslau. On the back she had written her husband's name and address at Rivesaltes. She tore the photo in half and gave the portion with the address on it to the aid worker.

"Keep this with him," she said. "It's his father's address. He might come back one day."

Mary took the baby in her arms and with a final farewell, walked back to the car.

Mary Elmes couldn't bring herself to go see the convoy leave the following morning. When her assistants returned from the camp later on, they were deeply distressed.

They had seen Helga Krauch mount the train with her little girl along with hundreds of other prisoners. Then, just before 7:00, when the train was due to depart, there was terrible screaming from further down the platform.

"It was a Belgian woman," said one of them. "She had come to the train with her two children to say good-bye to her husband. He was a Jew, but apparently she was not, and so she and the children were to be spared

from deportation. But the guards had discovered that there were three people missing from the number on the lists, and so they had seized her and her children and packed them into the train to make up numbers. She was screaming, 'I'm not Jewish! I'm not Jewish! These children are not Jewish!'"

Mary was horrified. "What did you do?" she gasped.

"We rushed down the platform and begged the guards to let the three of them get off the train. 'They're not Jewish,' we said. And do you know what the guards said?"

Mary shook her head.

"They said, 'Well, which three of you will make up the numbers, then?' And we were so ashamed. As if it would have been perfectly in order if the three of them had been Jewish! As if that would have made it okay!"

76

Mary was silent for a moment. She stared out of the window, imagining the scene only too well. Then she turned to her assistants.

"You'd better get your breakfast," she said. "You were up early this morning. You did all you could. Now, I'd better order food and drink for those poor people!"

She picked up the telephone and placed a call to the Toulouse office. When it was answered she said, "Happy sixtieth birthday, Alice!" and hung up.

The Toulouse receptionist replaced her receiver, rose from her chair and walked down the corridor to the canteen.

"They're on their way. Six hundred portions. You've got about two hours!"

Most of the caring organizations were allowed onto the platforms to bring food and drinks to the deportees on the trains. But the authorities did not give them sufficient warning of when the trains would arrive, nor how many people would need feeding. So, Mary had evolved a simple code. "Happy Birthday" meant that the train was on its way, and "sixty" in this case meant approximately 600 meals would be needed.

CHAPTER ELEVEN
Languedoc, France

Monday, September 14th, 1942

It was already getting hot and the train was moving very slowly along the track away from Rivesaltes. Helga Krauch held her daughter Lotte on her lap. Thankfully she was fast asleep. At least that made things easier. She wondered how she would manage when Lotte awoke and started asking for food or water. There were food supplies on the train, but she didn't know how or when they would be distributed. Fortunately, there was a toilet at the end of the corridor. The women and children were traveling in ordinary passenger coaches, dirty and in poor condition, but at least they were not being treated like cattle. She shuddered to think of the conditions in the boxcars at the front of the train where all the men were confined.

Although she didn't know it, for no news ever reached the inmates of Rivesaltes, the Archbishop of Toulouse had caused something of a stir a few days after the first convoy had passed through his city. He had been appalled to hear of the treatment of these unfortunate people, and had written a letter which had been read from every pulpit in the diocese the following Sunday. The letter read as follows:

> Women and children, fathers and mothers treated like cattle, members of a family separated from one another and dispatched to an unknown destination — it has been reserved for our own time to see such a sad spectacle. . . . The Jews are real men and women. Foreigners are real men and women. They cannot be abused without limit. . . . They are part of the human race. They are our brothers, like so many others.

The compartment was packed with women of all ages. Lotte was the only child — in fact there were only three other children under the age of ten on the train. Helga supposed that most of the other mothers had had the courage she lacked. They had given their children into the care of the various relief workers. Had she made a big mistake in refusing to part with Lotte?

The train was passing great lagoons on one side. There were strange birds wading in the shallow waters. She supposed they must be flamingos, they were so pink. Looking back the way they had come, she could see a range of mountains tumbling down to the sea, but they were becoming more distant now. It was a beautiful sight, and she wondered how such beauty could be so close to the filth and ugliness of the camp. Her thoughts were interrupted by the conversation around her. The women were arguing over their likely destination.

"One thing's certain," said one elderly lady, "they're not sending us to Spain! There's the Pyrenees over there, and we're traveling in the opposite direction. My husband and I got out of Germany in 1934 when things were getting tough for us Jews. We settled in France. We thought we'd make a new life there. Everybody knows that the French are a decent lot. There's no anti-Semitism in France! Then three years ago France was at

war with Germany, so they rounded us up and put us in a camp. Well, fair enough! We might have been spies or something, I suppose! Now that Germany has won the war, they're in charge in the north, but we're free down here in the south — or supposed to be — so you'd think they would let us slip over the border into Spain. Or maybe take us to Marseille and put us on a boat to America. Anything to keep us safe from the Nazis. But where are they taking us? Back to Germany, that's where! And you can guess what they'll do with us there…."

There was a general hubbub in the carriage as everybody tried to speak at once. As the noise died down, Helga realized that the train was stopping. Looking out of the window, she saw that the signs on the platform read Narbonne.

It had become very hot in the carriage, but the station awning provided some shade. The windows and doors were locked and there was no ventilation, so the halt in the station was most welcome. A few minutes later, the outdated engine which had been pulling the train slowly puffed past their window. Soon, there was a jolt as it was attached to their end of the train.

"I think they're going to take us back again!" *shouted someone.*

Sure enough, the train began to move back down the way it had just come. The fear of heading east towards Germany began to subside. But this time there were no lagoons or flamingos. Instead, they were passing between ranges of hills on either side. A youngish woman looked at the sun and made some calculations:

"We were heading north," *she said.* "Now we're going west."

There was a buzz of conversation. The West was better! The only countries west of France were Spain and Portugal. Or could they be going to a port on the west coast of France? Bordeaux, perhaps? But that coast was in

81

occupied France — in German hands! Waves of hope and fear succeeded each other. Was this good news or bad?

It was nearly 10:30 when the train stopped again. Many of the women had been dozing, but Lotte had woken up and started to cry. Her mother had her work cut out for her — trying to keep Lotte amused and comfortable. She had no toys with her, not even a doll or a teddy. They had only been allowed to bring a small bundle of spare clothing, and that was totally insufficient for more than a day or so.

Women were trying to get to the windows now to see what was going on. There was the sound of doors slamming, and the noise and smell of escaping steam and smoke showed that the engine was now only a few meters away from them.

On the platform, a small army of mostly women were pushing trollies towards the doors of the train, which were being opened by men in police uniforms.

"Where are we?" asked someone.

"Toulouse!" shouted the policeman who had just opened their door. "Now sit down and keep quiet. You're in luck, as these kind people have brought you some dinner."

Sure enough, a trolley of steaming rice appeared at the open door. Someone else came with mugs, tin plates, spoons, and jugs of water.

The policeman spotted Helga and Lotte and beckoned the mother to the door. After looking around the platform, he smiled at her, and then said in a low voice, "Are you still intending to keep your child with you?"

Helga was astonished at being addressed in this way. The officer obviously knew about her indecision. Or was it simply that she was almost the only mother on the train with a child?

Seeing that she didn't know how to reply, the policeman continued, "When you get to Montauban, the next stop, if you have changed your mind, have your little one ready and someone will be there to take her."

Helga found herself nodding wordlessly.

"It will have to be done quickly and without any fuss. I'll be at this door again, and one of these people will be there to look after her." He turned and waved a hand to indicate the helpers bustling about with trollies. "Trust us — it will be for the best!" With that, he turned and strode off down the platform.

The other women in the carriage had listened to this exchange in amazement. Their experiences at the hands of the French police had left them with nothing but fear and loathing. One young woman said in wonder, "There is some luck for you! Take it when you find it!"

83

Someone else said, "He must be connected with the Swiss Red Cross in some way."

"Or the Quakers," said someone sitting by the door.

She moved to allow Helga to take her place. "Sit here with your little girl. It will be easier for you when we get to Montauban."

"How long will that take, do you think?" asked Helga, taking her seat.

The general opinion of the carriage was that it shouldn't be much over half an hour — once they got going again.

Shortly after, there was a blast from the engine's whistle, and with a jolt the train rolled into motion. As the train pulled out of the station, Helga found the other half of the photo and tucked it inside Lotte's dress. She had no means of writing anything on the back of it this time.

The hand-over took place much more easily than anyone could have imagined. The train had stopped in Montauban, and Helga had sat with Lotte on her lap, not knowing what to expect or what to do. There was some commotion at the rear of the train where the men's boxcars were, and all attention was focused there.

At that moment the friendly policeman appeared with a beautiful Spanish doll in his hands. He held it out to Lotte, who in turn held out her arms to receive it. In a flash, she was in his arms. He whirled around still clutching the doll, and she disappeared into a group of helpers standing behind him. They melted away, and though Helga stared and stared to catch a glimpse of her, Lotte was gone.

84

With tears streaming down her face, Helga was comforted by the other women in the carriage.

"When she's older and she understands what you did and why you did it, she will thank you for it," one of them said.

The others agreed, and then fell silent as they contemplated what Lotte may have been saved from and what might still await them.

CHAPTER TWELVE
The Convoys

The Collinses were back at the Holocaust Museum in Paris the following morning. Earlier they had sat a long time over their breakfast considering the plans for the day. Dad said that although they needed to find out as much as they could about Grandad and his camp, they ought to find time to see Paris while they had the opportunity.

"I don't think we're going to find out much more anyway," agreed Andrew. "We spent ages going through those files on the computer yesterday, and apart from those two letters, we really found nothing else."

Emma disagreed. "What we did find though is really important. We know as sure as we can ever be that Grandad was in Rivesaltes, and that he was one of the children rescued by Mary Elmes. And what's more, we know that there were two of them."

"No, we don't," objected Andrew. "We only know that Mary *intended* to rescue two of them. We don't know that she actually did. And the fact that the Jewish organization only mentioned Franz suggests that something went wrong and the other child didn't make it."

"Do you know what I think?" said Mother, who had been silent until now.

"What do you think?" asked Dad.

"I think that we should have a talk with that nice French woman — Sabine, I think she was called. We should explain what we have found out and what we still need to know. She may have some idea of what we should do next."

The others thought that this was the best idea she had had since she took them to the BHV restaurant last night, and so that's what they did as soon as they had passed through security.

Sabine listened to their story and asked them a few questions.

"I don't think that there's much doubt," she said. "Mary Elmes took only one child. That seems pretty certain. What happened to the other one? Almost certainly the mother changed her mind and refused to part with him or her. We see many examples of this in the records we have here. Mothers simply couldn't believe that their children would be better off with strangers than under their own protection. But of course, they had no idea of what was in store for them."

"So you think that our Grandad had a brother or a sister who died in Auschwitz?" asked Emma. "That's terrible!"

"Well, all the survivors of the Shoah lost members of their families, and there are many examples of brothers and sisters being separated — some to survive and some to perish. But if you really want to know the truth about your ancestor, we can probably find out for you right now. Do you want me to go ahead?"

The Collinses looked at each other in consternation. They had not expected this.

Emma spoke first. "Well, it's your aunt or uncle we're talking about, Dad! Do you want to know?"

Everyone looked at Dad. He took a deep breath and nodded. "Go on, please," he said.

Sabine led them to a desk and arranged seats for them. Then she fired up the computer and typed something on the keyboard. Turning to them she asked, "Have you heard of the Klarsfelds?"

They shook their heads.

"No," said Mr. Collins. "Should we?"

"Probably not if all this is new to you," smiled Sabine. "Serge and Beate Klarsfeld have done a tremendous amount of research in tracing the French Jews who perished in the Shoah. Particularly the children. They have identified over 11,000 children. They wanted them to be known as individuals, not just as 'eleven thousand,' and so they have listed them by name with their last known address. In the case of two and a half thousand of them, they even have their pictures. And they want surviving relatives to help them find pictures of the rest of them."

All this time, Sabine was typing on the keyboard. She turned to the family who had left their seats and were crowding around her.

"Look!" she said, "Here you are. This is convoy number thirty-three from Drancy. This convoy included all those who had just arrived from Rivesaltes on convoy number five. You see, it says here: 'Camp of Rivesaltes — 571 names. This group arrived at Drancy from Rivesaltes on September 15.' That's a couple of days after your grandfather was rescued. You see here it tells you what room in Drancy they were held in. And if we click on this...we get a list of all the children on the convoy." She scrolled down to the *K*'s. "And there's no Krauch! So your Grandad's brother or sister didn't die at Auschwitz!"

"Wow," said Andrew, "that's something! So what do you think happened?"

"Maybe the mother changed her mind. There might have been an opportunity which presented itself before they reached the German-occupied zone. After that it would have been too late."

"So you think Grandad's brother or sister might have survived after all?" asked Andrew.

"It's certainly possible."

"And what about Grandad's mother?"

"Well, Serge Klarsfeld has only listed the children here. We need to go elsewhere to find the names of the adult victims." She was about to type in something else, but Emma stopped her.

"Just a minute!" she said. "Not all of those children in the list have got addresses. There's just a blank space. Why is that?"

"Good point!" replied Sabine. "But do you see the assembly point for most of them? They're from Rivesaltes! That *was* their last known address! Most of the others for whom we do have addresses were assembled at Drancy, and there are records of where they were taken from, their actual home address, here in Paris."

Emma looked puzzled. "What is Drancy?"

Sabine smiled. "Another good question! But let's find your great-grandmother first! We need to go to our database. Here, look! 'Search for a person.' What was her name?"

"We don't know her first name," said Mr. Collins. "Just her surname: Krauch."

"Okay! Could be tricky if there are several. Let's try.... Oh, there you are then. Just one! Read it for yourselves."

Andrew leaned forward and said, "It's all in French!"

Sabine smiled again. "Sorry, I forgot. I'll translate. It says: 'Madame Helga Krauch, born 17th January 1914 at Breslau. Deported to Auschwitz by the convoy number 33 departing from Drancy 16th September, 1942.'"

"So she did die then?" asked Andrew.

"Almost certainly. I'm sorry. But I think that you guessed that. Anyway, you have her name now. That will help you in your research. Helga Krauch from Breslau!"

"Where is Breslau?" asked Dad. "Is it in Germany?"

"It was then. Now it's part of Poland and it's called Wroclaw. But you were asking about Drancy?"

"Yes," said Emma. "You said something about them being assembled in Drancy."

"Drancy is a suburb of Paris," replied Sabine. "Just before the war they started to build a new housing estate of high-rise apartements there. It was going to be called *La Cité de la Muette* — The Silent City — because it was supposed to become a place of peace and rest. But under the German occupation it became a sort of holding pen for all the people known as 'undesirables,' which of course included all the Jews. Terrible things happened there. Fortunately, it seems that your Helga was only there for one night, although the journey east must have been terrible too."

"Is it still there?" asked Mrs. Collins.

"It is, and people live in those buildings today. But there are memorials and a museum. If you have time, I think you should go there."

"Shall we?" asked Emma, looking at her father.

"We said that we should take the opportunity to see more of Paris," he replied. "Perhaps this is what we should do this afternoon. We've got the rest of the day free! How do we get there?"

Sabine explained the best way of getting to Drancy, and promised to keep her eyes open for any more information which might lead to finding Grandad's missing brother or sister.

Cobh

Cork

Wall of names, Paris Shoah Memorial

Wall of the Righteous, Paris Shoah Memorial

Research room at the Shoah Memorial

"I know just where to look. It's somewhere in that main road called the 'BHV', the Bazar de l'Hôtel de Ville."

Drancy, memorial to the victims of the camp

Drancy, its train tracks and the replica of a wagon used for prisoner deportation

Argelès Retirada Memorial

Collioure, its stretching steps by the castle

Memorials to the various groups of victims interned in the Rivesaltes camp

The inside of one the Rivesaltes camp barracks

Rivesaltes latrines

Ramp down to the Rivesaltes Memorial Museum entrance

Ron Friend: the child who was the inspiration for this novel

Spanish refugees at the Argelès camp
(Photo courtesy of Chauvin, Argelès Camp Memorial)

The renovated maternity at Elne

Some of the Retirada pictures exhibited at the maternity

Mary Elmes at a feeding station in Almería
(Photo courtesy of motherjones175.files.wordpress)

*Avenue des Baléares, where
Mary Elmes lived in Perpignan*

*Mary Elmes Bridge:
Inauguration*

CHAPTER THIRTEEN
Drancy

Getting to Drancy sounded complicated, and the Collinses were hungry, so Mrs. Collins led them back up to the *Bazar de l'Hôtel de Ville* — the BHV — where they knew they could find food and rest. After eating, Andrew and his Dad pored over a *Métro* map and tried to follow the instructions they had been given, while Emma and her mother had a last look around the store.

"We need to take the *Métro* to *République*, and change there," said Mr. Collins. "Then we take this one as far as…where did she say we had to get off?"

"*Porte de Pantin*," Andrew replied. "Right there! Then we have to take bus number 151 as far as *Avenue Jean Jaurès*. That sounds simple enough."

When they were all together again, they set off for Drancy. Emma was thinking about Grandad's mother who had also made this journey.

Like her, they didn't know what they were going to find when they got there. But unlike her they could come and go as they wanted!

Everything worked out fine. They emerged from the *Métro* to find the 151 bus waiting, and soon they were on their way up a long straight road that seemed to go on and on forever. Actually, it was only about twenty minutes before the digital display told them that the next stop was *Avenue Jean Jaurès*. When they got off the bus, they found themselves on a suburban crossroads in a rather shabby district.

"It's this way," announced Andrew, leading the way around the corner. On their right was a large parking lot and just ahead on the left they could see a grassy space. When they got nearer, they realized that they had reached their destination.

102 Beyond the grass was a large rectangular area with trees and benches. Surrounding this open space was an open rectangle of apartment buildings — the two longer sides on their left and right, and in the distance the shorter side joining the other two. The apartment buildings stood four stories high with a covered terrace below them. They looked to be in reasonable condition, and were obviously inhabited. This could have been any elderly suburban housing estate, but what made it different was the fact that in the center of the open end of the rectangle there were railway tracks. On these tracks stood one solitary cattle wagon.

"What does it say on that wagon?" asked Mrs. Collins.

The words were written in French and faded with age, but their meaning was clear.

"It says 'ten horses, or forty men,'" said Andrew.

So this is what took them to the death camps, thought Emma. She looked around her. People were going about their business without a second glance at the wagon. *They must pass it every day*, she thought. *Does it mean anything to them after all this time?*

Several commemorative plaques were set in the ground near the wagon, in French of course, and the two youngsters struggled to translate them.

"This one was placed here in 1993, the fiftieth anniversary of what happened here," said Andrew. "It says that thousands of Jews, Gypsies, and foreigners were sent from here to the Nazi camps, where nearly all of them died."

They were trying to translate another notice some distance away near the edge of the area when an elderly man stopped and asked them if they needed any help.

"We are finding it a bit difficult to understand," said Emma. "We know this has something to do with a tunnel but we don't understand what the tunnel was for."

"This notice marks the route of an escape tunnel," he said. "Let me translate it for you. It says: 'Underneath this pathway, at a depth of one and a half meters, is the escape tunnel of the Drancy camp. Seventy prisoners, in three teams, worked day and night to complete it. Commenced in September, 1943, it was thirty-six meters long when it was discovered by the Nazis in November 1943 and was never finished. They were just three meters from liberty!'"

"How awful!" said Mrs. Collins. "Just three meters away from freedom. I wonder what happened to them."

"I don't understand," said Emma, looking around. "This isn't like I imagined at all. This is just three blocks of apartments. Surely they could walk out anytime!"

The man smiled sadly. "I'm afraid it wasn't that easy," he said. "There was barbed wire enclosing the whole area, and there were watch towers at each corner. These apartments were built to hold 700 people, but at times there were over seven *thousand* held here. Not just in the apartments, of course, but all over this open space, which had no grass or trees then — just concrete. Sometimes there were fifty people sleeping in one room! They were in bunk beds, two or more to a bed. They were on the floor under the beds, on the tables, on the stairs and landings. And no proper place to wash or to use the toilet. Altogether, almost 100,000 people — men, women, and children — passed through here, and only 1,518 survived. You can read that on the memorial over there." He turned and pointed back to the way they had come in.

"I'm sorry, I don't mean to be rude, but I find it hard to imagine fifty people sleeping in one room," said Mrs. Collins.

The old man smiled ruefully. "I'm sorry, I should have explained better! These apartments were not finished when all those people were imprisoned here. The interior walls had not been completed, so the spaces inside were more like dormitories than rooms. Even so, the overcrowding was terrible. And there was no electricity or water at first. The first batch of prisoners was left without food or water for several days. And there were many deaths and suicides. Conditions improved gradually, but they were always shocking. On a few occasions, prisoners were taken at random and shot in retaliation for the activities of the Resistance."[9]

Mrs. Collins shook her head in dismay that such things could have happened to innocent people in a civilized city like Paris.

---

[9] The Resistance was comprised of many groups of people who fought the Germans and the collaborationist Vichy government during the Nazi occupation of France.

"Do you have any personal interest in this place?" their new friend asked.

Mr. Collins answered for them all. "Yes. My grandmother was here. She was brought here from Rivesaltes. We are going to visit that camp soon."

"Ah well, this place will mean something to you then. For most who pass by, it's just a bit of history that's best forgotten. And for others, it's something they don't want here at all. Ten years ago, someone painted a swastika on that wagon. And there used to be more wagons here, but they were burned twelve years ago. But it's not all bad! A few years ago, they opened a new museum — it's over the road there — that concrete and glass building. But like many things in Paris, it's closed for the August holidays. You must come back when it's open."

They thanked the old man for his help and went over to look at the memorial, a huge concrete column depicting an imprisoned family, with two other columns surrounding it — which their friend had told them represented the doors of death closing in on the family.

"I just can't believe what's happened to us in the past few weeks," murmured Mother. "A month ago, we knew nothing of this. Now, thanks to Emma's homework, we've discovered so much about Grandad's family — and about ourselves."

"We need to get in touch with Grandad and tell him what we have found out here in Paris," said Andrew. "If only he would learn how to text or use WhatsApp."

His father answered. "I don't think there's much sense in bothering him now. There's so much to tell him he wouldn't remember it all, and then he'd be confused, wondering exactly what we'd said. I think the best thing is to write a letter as soon as we get to the campsite."

"I want to tell him that he's got a brother or sister!" exclaimed Emma.

Her father shook his head. "It's too soon for that," he said. We don't know anything for sure yet. It's unlikely that he or she is still alive, and even if they are, we will probably never know."

"Just like Grandad's father," added Mrs. Collins. "We know that he was taken away somewhere, but we don't know where."

They stayed a little longer, taking photos to show Grandad, and trying to take it all in. Then, knowing that tomorrow was going to be a very long day indeed, they took the bus and the *Métro* back to where they were staying.

CHAPTER FOURTEEN
Argelès-sur-Mer

The journey from Paris to Argelès-sur-Mer was something of an ordeal. The Collinses began to regret not planning two days for it — but at least the children were old enough to amuse themselves without the constant "Are we there yet?" protests, like they used to do. The parents took turns driving, stopping every couple of hours at rest areas, while Emma and Andrew passed the time by reading, watching the scenery pass by, and, of course, spending long sessions on their mobile devices.

Emma had stopped checking WhatsApp, as she found the remarks made by her so-called friends increasingly irritating. She had become so involved in the search for the truth about her grandfather's family — *her* family, she reminded herself — that the situation with John Braddock, and her friends' reaction to it, seemed stupid and childish. She was still deeply moved by what she had learned yesterday about the conditions in Drancy all those years ago, and had no time at all for the silliness of the girls back home. *Perhaps I'm growing up,* she thought. *Is this what being an adult means?*

They were driving on higher ground now. The countryside had changed and a sign announced that they were in the Auvergne. *Région des Volcans* it said. Emma wondered if the volcanoes were still active. Just then her phone beeped with a text message. She didn't send or receive texts very often since most people messaged on Instagram and WhatsApp. It was from John Braddock. *Oh no! Now what?*

But it was alright. It was short and sensible. He said that he had heard about the comments circulating among their classmates, that he was sorry if he was to blame in any way, and that he hoped that she was having success with her research.

Emma smiled to herself. It was typical of him, she thought. He really was quite a nice guy. The others just hadn't had the opportunity to get to know him better like she had. She settled back in her seat and composed a short reply, bringing him up to date with the main discoveries they had made in Paris.

Andrew, who had been studying the map on his iPhone, announced that they were about to cross the Millau Viaduct, which, he said, was a bridge taller than the Eiffel Tower. This was met with some disbelief, but this soon turned to amazement as they found themselves soaring above the valley, suspended in the air by what seemed to be the flimsiest of steel ropes! Unfortunately they had already passed the viewing area on the northern side of the valley, but Dad promised that they would stop on the way back to take photographs. As it was, they pulled into the first service area they saw after the crossing.

Emma and Andrew wandered off to look around the shops, having agreed to meet up for drinks in fifteen minutes. When they all sat down together, Dad had some news for everybody.

"I got a phone call," he said, "from Sabine at the museum in Paris. She found out about our missing child. It was a girl!"

"You mean Grandad had a sister, then?" asked Andrew.

"That's right. She was taken off the train at a station called Montauban, apparently with her mother's consent. She was then taken to Toulouse, to a children's home called the *Château de Larade*."

"Wow," said Emma. "So she survived; she could still be alive! That's your auntie, Dad!"

"Hold on, hold on! Not so fast. They don't know anything more than that, except for her name. She was called Lotte."

"But don't they know what happened to her after that?" asked Mother.

"Apparently not. This so-called *château* wasn't a grand castle or anything like that, it was just an old, run-down building that the Archbishop of Toulouse had lent to the Quakers to help them look after the Spanish children."

109

"What Spanish children?" asked Emma.

"From the Spanish Civil War," answered Dad.

"But Grandad's sister was German! So why did they put her with a load of Spanish children?"

"That's what l wanted to know! Apparently it was all part of a cunning plan. She was Jewish, of course, and in danger; so she needed to have a new identity. She was not old enough to understand that she had to become a different person, and they were afraid that she would give herself away if she was placed in an ordinary home. So she was hidden among the Spanish children."

"And then what happened to her?" asked Mother again.

"That's what they don't know. She would have been given a Spanish name, and quite soon would have been speaking Spanish. We may never know what became of her. Many of those children were adopted by Spanish families. Some went back to Spain later on, but many stayed in France."

"So is that what happened to Grandad, too?" asked Andrew.

"No, he was so much younger — he was only about six months old. It would have been easy to place him with a French family when the time came."

"When what time came?"

"Well, only a few weeks after Grandad was rescued, the Germans invaded the non-occupied south of France, and all the remaining Jews were rounded up. That's when he would have been hidden with some friendly French family. There's still so much we don't know, and perhaps never will."

At that moment, a waiter came with a tray of coffees and cokes, and the family sat drinking and thinking in silence.

They arrived in Argelès-sur-Mer by the early evening and followed signs to the campsite near the beach.

"Here we are," said Mother. "Just there on the left! *Camping Sud.*"

Her husband brought the car to a stop at the gate, applied the hand-brake, and jumped out of the vehicle. Emma wondered how he would manage with the little French he had, but he seemed to be speaking well enough with someone inside the cabin. Then he emerged with a ring of keys.

"Do tents have keys?" Andrew asked, puzzled.

The two adults exchanged amused glances. Dad said nothing, and drove slowly through the camp. They passed tents of all colors, shapes and sizes, and then turning behind a hedge, they saw what appeared to be a little neighborhood of bungalows.

They pulled up in front of a large mobile home with a terrace and a small, attractive garden surrounded by a low wooden fence.

"Wow!" exclaimed Andrew. "Some tent!"

Dad laughed. "Mum and I didn't like the idea of a tent," he said, "even a luxury one! This seemed to be the best of both worlds."

111

They were soon inside the mobile home and exploring what it had to offer. Emma was delighted with her bedroom as was Andrew with his. The kitchen was spotless and equipped with everything they could possibly need. The bathroom easily passed Mum's inspection, and both youngsters were impressed with the iPhone dock beside the TV.

"You two go off and explore the site while we unpack," suggested their mother.

They couldn't miss the swimming pool — it was huge! In fact it was three pools, connected together in what was described as "California style." But what attracted them most was the beach — directly accessible from the campsite. It was a vast expanse of sand, in one direction stretching away out of sight, and in the other towards the distant mountains. There were a surprising number of people still about; some sunbathing, some swimming, some playing beach volleyball. Yet the expanse of sand was so huge that the beach still seemed almost empty. Emma thought of the beach back home in Cobh, and shook her head in awe.

By the time they had unpacked and settled in, it was getting quite late. They had eaten fairly well on the journey down, so they decided to make do with takeout. Emma and Andrew were sent to the bar with enough euros for a pizza and some drinks.

A guy behind the counter smiled as they approached and said, "What can I do for you?"

Emma wondered, *how is it that everyone knows we speak English?* but she said nothing while Andrew placed the order.

"Just arrived?" asked the teenaged boy counting out the change from the till.

"An hour or so ago," replied Emma. And feeling bold as he seemed friendly, she asked, "Are you French? You speak very good English!"

He smiled, his white teeth set in a very sun-tanned face. "Spanish French," he answered.

Andrew looked puzzled, but said nothing.

The boy noticed that they were both somewhat confused by his answer, so he explained, "Many people here come from Spanish families but were born here in France, so we're French."

"Oh," said Emma, still not much the wiser. "What language do you speak at home then?"

"French with my mother, but Catalan with my dad and grandfather," replied the boy. And then, seeing that they looked even more confused, he broke into laughter.

"Catalan is the local language on both sides of the Pyrenees!" He pointed to the mountains where the sun was already low in the sky. "Around here we're all Catalan first and foremost, and then either Spanish or French second."

"Your English is so good!" Emma marveled again.

"That's because so many of our customers are English! Okay — here's your pizza, and your drinks. Can you manage them?"

Emma and Andrew assured him that they could and said together, "Good night!"

"*À bientôt!*" he replied. "That means, 'See you soon!'"

I hope so, thought Emma.

CHAPTER FIFTEEN
Pierre

The following morning Emma woke up early. She pulled back the blinds of the little bedroom window and peeked out. The sun was already up, and there were several people passing by their mobile home. She quickly pulled on some shorts and a top and tiptoed out of the room. All was silent; nobody seemed to be stirring.

Emma let herself out quietly and made her way toward the beach. It was a beautiful morning. There were a few vacationers about, but Emma felt that she had the beach almost all to herself. The sun was climbing out of the sea, its rays reflecting over the water in a shimmering pathway from the horizon to her feet as she walked towards the shore. To her right, the mountains seemed to rise up out of the sea and climb higher and higher until they disappeared into the wispy clouds in the far distance. There was one particularly big mountain out there with what might have been just a streak of snow near the summit, its lower slopes covered with patches of green — no doubt forests of some kind, thought Emma. She turned around slowly, taking in the whole sparkling scene before her. She found her eyes kept coming back to the great mountain in the distance. She wondered if people climbed it, and whether there was a road up to its summit.

Behind her was the camp with its pines, and beyond she could see rows of palm trees leading towards the town. It was hot already, and she realized that she hadn't taken any precautions against the sun. There was a small building a short distance away that cast a long shadow across the sand. She moved towards it to take advantage of its shade, and noticed too late that there was already someone there. The sun, low in the sky, had temporarily blinded her.

"Hi there!" said a voice, somehow familiar. "*Ça va?*"

It was the boy from the bar they had spoken to last night. He had been looking at the mountains through a pair of binoculars, which he lowered as he saw her approach.

She realized immediately who it was, but didn't know how to reply. What did *ça va* mean? She smiled and said rather lamely, "Hello."

"All alone? No boyfriend this morning?"

Emma frowned. *No boyfriend? What's he talking about?* Then she realized. "Oh! Last night. That was my brother, Andrew!"

The boy laughed. "Sorry, my mistake! I'm Pierre, by the way. What's your name?"

Emma told him, and then because she couldn't think of anything else to say, she added, "What were you looking at?"

Pierre smiled again and pointed to the mountain.

"Canigou," he said.

"Is that the name of that mountain?" asked Emma.

"Yes, this is the best time of the day to look at it. It's lit up by the sun now. Later in the day it's in the shade."

"Can you climb it?" asked Emma, and then she added hastily, "I mean, can it be climbed?"

Pierre laughed again. "Yes, it's quite easy to climb, if you're fit. And yes, I've climbed it many times."

"Could I do it?"

"You can take a jeep taxi up most of the way. Then it's about a two-hour climb." He looked Emma up and down and added, grinning, "You look fit enough to me!"

Emma saw that he was being playful, but she didn't know whether to be pleased or offended, so she just replied, "We don't have any mountains that size where I come from!"

"Where do you come from?" asked Pierre.

"Ireland. A place called Cobh. It used to be Queenstown. It's near Cork."

"Oh! So you're not English! I assumed that everyone who spoke English was English or American."

Emma laughed. "Or Australian or Canadian," she teased.

"Well, you can tell their accents are different from English people," said Pierre, "but yours sounds just the same."

"I don't think anybody in England would agree with you," smiled Emma. "But it's true that my accent isn't as strong as many Irish people. Have you ever been there?"

"No, I've never been to Ireland. But I've been to England. I was there last year. There was an exchange with an English school in Suffolk. I spent nearly a month there. I suppose that's where I picked up most of my English. And then this Easter, some of the students at that school came here and stayed with us, so I've had plenty of opportunities to practice the language. I hope to go back again sometime, but I don't have any plans at the moment." Then before she could think of anything else to say, he asked, "What about your French?"

118 Emma made a face. "Not good, I'm afraid. We've got a really good teacher at school, but I suppose I don't work as hard at it as I should. Art's my best subject."

"Is this your first time here?"

"To Argelès, yes. We've been to Paris a couple of times, but we usually go to Greece." She went on to tell him about the disappointment with the vacation in Santorini.

"So what made you pick Argelès-sur-Mer?" asked Pierre.

"It's a long story." replied Emma, realizing that she ought to get back for breakfast, and not wanting to bore this rather interesting young man with her grandfather's history.

"Well, keep it till later!" suggested Pierre. "How about in the bar later this morning? I'm off duty today. Let me buy you a coke!"

Emma was embarrassed. She didn't know what to say. "I don't know what my parents have planned," she said. "But if we're around, I might be able to. But you don't have to buy me anything!"

Pierre laughed again. *"À bientôt,"* he said. "Remember what that means?"

"See you soon," she answered. And she laughed, too.

When she got back the others were already at breakfast.

"Where have you been?" demanded her mother angrily. "Nobody had the slightest idea where you had gone!"

"Sorry, Mum," said Emma. She didn't know what to say about her unexpected encounter on the beach, so she just mumbled something about getting some air and exercise.

119

"She was cooped up in a car all day yesterday," Dad said, coming to his daughter's defense as usual. But seeing his wife's face he added, "But you should have told someone where you were going."

"There was no one to tell!" insisted Emma.

"Leave a note then," said Dad.

"Sorry, Mum. Sorry, Dad. It won't happen again! It's gorgeous out there, by the way."

"You didn't wear your sunhat either," complained her mother.

Andrew looked at his sister and rolled his eyes. He also wondered what she had been up to, but said nothing.

The family quickly decided that after yesterday's mammoth journey, today should be a quiet one. By 10:00 they were all comfortably seated by the pool in their swimsuits. Mother was reading a woman's magazine and Dad soon fell asleep. The kids splashed around in the water awhile, and then Emma suggested they go for drinks. They dried themselves, put on T-shirts, and walked over to the bar. They bought two cokes and a bag of chips and sat down under a large umbrella. Pierre, who had been sitting some distance away watching the family at the pool, now got up and strolled across to where they were sitting.

"Mind if I join you?" he asked.

Andrew looked surprised, then annoyed. But Emma quickly came to the rescue. "This is my brother Andrew," she said, "and this is Pierre, Andrew!"

Pierre watched Andrew's face with amusement. "Remember me from last night?" he prompted. "Emma and I spoke this morning."

Andrew just nodded, trying to take it all in. Was this a chance meeting, or had his sister arranged it?

There was a moment's awkward silence, and then Pierre said, "Emma was going to tell me what brought you to Argelès!"

Emma felt that it was up to her to tell the story.

"Well, it was all to do with our grandfather," she said. And she began to tell Pierre about the photo with the writing and the camp in Rivesaltes. Pierre interrupted once or twice to ask questions. He didn't seem to be bored, Andrew noticed.

"Have you heard of this place — Rivesaltes?" Andrew asked Pierre.

"Oh yes," he replied. "It's in the news a lot right now. But it wasn't always like that. Just a few years ago they were going to flatten what was left of it, and hardly anybody cared. Now they're all talking about the new museum that was recently built there. Are you planning to visit it?"

"Yes, that's why we're here. Today we're just resting from the journey, and tomorrow I guess we'll be trying to find our way there. We've only got a week here, so we need to get on with it as soon as possible. Is it easy to find?"

"You really need someone to act as a guide and show you round," answered Pierre. "If you can wait a day or two longer, I might be able to fix something up. One of my teachers belongs to a group of people who have been fighting for some time to get a proper memorial and museum for Rivesaltes. I'm sure I can arrange for one of them to meet you and take you there. They know just about all there is to know about the place!"

"That would be great," said Emma. "Thank you very much. You'd better meet our parents so that we can arrange something in a day or two."

"In the meantime," said Pierre, "there's quite a lot to know about Argelès, too. Do you fancy a short guided tour?"

"Later, perhaps. But right now I think we'd better get back to Mum and Dad." She collected their glasses and plates and carried them over to the bar.

She turned and smiled at him. "*À bientôt,*" she said.

Pierre smiled back. "*À bientôt,*" he replied.

Back at the pool, the youngsters joined their parents.

"Dad was saying that we should find this place tomorrow," said Mum, looking up from her magazine.

"I think we should wait a day or two," said Emma. "We've been talking to a boy who offered to find someone to take us there and explain everything to us."

"Is that really necessary?" asked her father. "Don't forget, we've only got a week here. Won't there be guides at the camp? And leaflets we can take away — that sort of thing?"

"Maybe. Apparently there's a museum there now, but of course it may all be in French."

122 "Who is this boy, and what does he know about it?" Mother asked.

"He works here at the bar. He's called Pierre. It's just a summer job; he's still in school. He's going to come and see you once he's arranged something."

"Is he English?" asked Dad. "You seem to have been able to speak with him okay."

"No, he's French, or Spanish — it's a bit complicated. But he speaks very good English. He seems really nice."

"He's got Emma speaking French now," said her brother. "I think we need to watch her; there's something going on there!"

She sighed. On the whole, she got on pretty well with her brother. But sometimes he just couldn't resist teasing her. Had he really noticed anything? She decided to play it cool.

"Grow up, Andrew! He's just someone who could be very helpful to us. That's all."

Her father looked at his wife and raised his eyebrows. She shook her head and put her finger to her lips. Neither of them said anything.

CHAPTER SIXTEEN
The Argelès Camp

The following morning, the Collinses were up early — or what they thought was early. However, they had forgotten that France was an hour ahead of Ireland, and although they had set their watches to French time, their internal clocks had remained on Irish time. They were surprised to find that it was already nearly 9:00.

Mr. Collins was keen to visit the Rivesaltes camp as soon as possible, and was somewhat irritated to find that his daughter did not share his enthusiasm. "After all, that's the only reason we came here!" he exclaimed.

"Yes Dad, I know," she answered. "And I want to go there, too. We all do! But as I told you yesterday, it would be much better to wait until Pierre's friend is available. We'll find out so much more that way. Especially since we're not too good at French."

He sighed. He always seemed to be outnumbered by the rest of the family. However, there might be some sense in what his daughter was saying. "So what do you suggest we do today?"

Mrs. Collins thought it was time they had a look at the town of Argelès and suggested so. "After all, we had a pretty quiet day yesterday," she said.

It was already getting quite warm, so dressed appropriately for a hot, sunny day, the family set off along the promenade towards the center of town. To their left was the wide, flat expanse of the beach. Already families were setting up umbrellas and making themselves comfortable in light-weight reclining chairs, ready for a day of sunbathing and relaxation.

On the other side of the promenade there were hotels and houses with gardens bursting with color. Blue, purple, and orange seemed to predominate, and neither Mr. nor Mrs. Collins knew the names of all of the exotic shrubs. There were magnificent palm trees too, giving a welcome shade from the already burning sun.

Further on they entered a section of the path that passed through an area of pine trees; it was much cooler here and there was a pleasant fresh smell from the trees. A large colorful notice board drew their attention. They struggled to understand the French until Andrew spotted the English translation provided below it. "It says that the pines were planted here about a hundred years ago to stop the sand from being blown away. But at various times many of them have been destroyed for different reasons — during the war, for example. Now they are being protected."

Now that they were getting towards the more populated area, there were rather tatty children's playgrounds with giant plastic animals to clamber over, and the inevitable bouncy castle. Emma thought that once upon a time she would have loved that, but now it all seemed rather tasteless and out of keeping with the splendid beach and distant mountains. She found herself wondering what Pierre thought about the tourists and their pleasures. Did he find them intrusive, she wondered? Then she remembered that he earned his pocket money by working in the bar, so he couldn't be totally against them. Yet somehow he didn't seem to fit into this foreign holiday atmosphere. He was so proud of his Spanish (or was it Catalan?) roots, that she doubted whether he really enjoyed the summer, and was probably glad when they all went home and peace descended on the town again.

"So what do you think, Emma?" asked her mother rather sharply. Evidently Emma had missed something because of her daydreaming.

"Sorry, what were you saying?"

"I said, what about a ride on this?" Her mother was pointing at a picture of a sort of road train — several wagons with seats pulled by a vehicle rather crudely disguised as a railway engine. It reminded Emma of Thomas the Tank Engine, and she wasn't particularly impressed.

"It'll give us a chance to sit down," her mother went on, "it's shady, and it'll be cool as it's all open to the air. I don't know about the rest of you, but I need a sit-down! It's one way of seeing the town without having to walk in this heat."

Indeed, it was getting really hot, especially as they were now out of the shady pine trees. Emma realized that she was going to have to make a decision, so she quickly agreed to the idea. Andrew spotted a wooden building just ahead, which seemed to be the booking office for what appeared to be called the "train-bus." Fortunately, the man behind the counter spoke English — as did most of the people they had had to deal with so far — and they soon possessed a family ticket for the full tour, which would last an hour.

"You want the orange train, and it will be here in ten minutes," explained the man in the ticket office. In fact it was nearly twenty minutes before the train arrived and disgorged a load of vacationers before allowing the family to climb on board.

It was an interesting trip. They bounced along the roads at an impressive speed for such a small and vulnerable vehicle. Emma could see that her mother might be regretting her choice of amusement. They paid a quick visit to the port with its assortment of grand yachts, and then turned inland to an old quarter of the town which Emma realized was probably the original village. The rest of the way they passed innumerable campsites, all much like their own, all with their own pools and restaurants — making it so that customers need never leave the camp to find food, shelter, or entertainment.

128

But that isn't why we are here, thought Emma. *We are here for a purpose*, and that was to discover the truth behind Grandad's faded picture and the writing on the back. What a lot had happened since she had first picked it off the floor in Grandad's living room!

But she was daydreaming again. Mum was saying something about the trip — she was disappointed about something apparently.

"What did you say?" asked Emma.

"I said, it's a pity there is no commentary on what we are seeing. I was hoping we would learn something more about this place."

Emma remembered that Pierre had offered to show her around some time, but decided not to mention that just now, so she just replied, "Well, you probably wouldn't have heard anything anyway. With so much road noise it's difficult enough to hear each other speak."

"And it would have been in French," Dad pointed out.

"I do like to know something about the history of a place," said his wife. "What was this place like before all the visitors started coming? And what was it like here during the war, I wonder?"

They all agreed that these were interesting questions to which they would like answers. Emma thought that she knew where these answers might be found, but she kept this information to herself. She smiled as she thought of Pierre and what she would tell him of this morning's trip when they next met.

They decided to get off the train before the tour ended. Dad had recognized the avenue they were bouncing down, and realized that in a few moments they would be passing the entrance to *Le Sud* — their campsite. So when it stopped further on, they got off and strolled back to the camp entrance. By now it was lunchtime, and as they were feeling too hot and lazy to prepare any food themselves, they made a quick visit to the bathroom and then wandered over to the bar for something to eat and drink.

129

Emma looked around, rather hoping that Pierre would come and serve them, but it seemed that he was not on duty. They ordered their snack from a young woman who, rather surprisingly, did not seem to understand English — so they ordered by pointing to the pictures on the menu board.

After lunch, Mother announced that she was going for a nap, while Dad made another attempt at getting the espresso machine to work. Not that they needed any — they'd just had cokes in the bar — but he had a fascination with gadgets and didn't want to be beaten.

That left the two teenagers to themselves. They were both in the same frame of mind, so within minutes they were changed into swimsuits and headed for the pool.

It was an hour or so before the two of them returned to the mobile home (or bungalow — Emma couldn't make up her mind what the right description was) to find, to their surprise, Pierre sitting next to their father on the terrace.

"Hi, you two!" called Dad. "You've got a visitor. Your friend came over a few minutes ago. He's got some news about our visit to the Rivesaltes camp. I told him to take a seat — that you wouldn't be long."

"Hi Pierre," said Emma, rather embarrassed to be caught in her bikini by someone she hardly knew. "I'll just get changed." She hastily disappeared into her room, leaving her brother on the terrace to continue the conversation.

"Your father was telling me about the train-bus trip you had this morning. What did you think of Argelès?" asked Pierre.

"Well, it's very different from where we usually go in Greece," said Andrew. "I don't think it's the sort of place we'd have come to if we hadn't had a good reason."

"You didn't like it then?" inquired Pierre.

Before Andrew could think of a suitable reply that wouldn't offend Pierre, Dad said hastily, "This time of the year it's obviously full of tourists. It's probably very different out of season."

Pierre nodded. "It's very different in the winter. In early September when the weather is still perfect there are hardly any tourists about, and most of the campsites are almost deserted. Some are even closed completely. You wouldn't recognize the place. Did you learn anything about the history of Argelès?"

At this point, Emma reappeared wearing a smart dress. She had recovered her composure and entered the conversation. "We read something about the pine trees. When they were planted, and how from time to time they were cut down."

"Did you understand who cut them down and why?" asked Pierre.

"Wasn't it something about the war?" replied Emma.

"Which war?" Pierre asked, and then suddenly apologized. "I'm sorry I'm starting to sound like my school teacher! I shouldn't be putting you through all this. It's just that it's hard for us who care about what happened here, to see people totally unaware of the terrible things that happened on these beaches. We find it hard to keep quiet. We think that there should be a more visible memorial, just like there is now at Rivesaltes."

The Collinses looked at one another in concern. Had they been guilty of some thoughtless remark, which had obviously upset Pierre? What did he mean about terrible things happening on the beaches? And what did it have to do with Rivesaltes? They looked at Emma to answer. He was her friend, after all.

"We know that Rivesaltes was a concentration camp," said Emma, "and that awful things happened there. That's why we're here. To find out about our Grandad. But we don't know anything about this place. How was this like Rivesaltes?"

"Argelès too had a concentration camp, before Rivesaltes. And many would say that it was worse — far worse. But in a different way, perhaps."

Emma gasped and put her hand to her mouth. "How stupid I've been!" she said. "Of course I know what you are talking about! This must have been the beach where all the Spanish refugees were herded onto after they crossed the mountains in February 1939. This was where Mary Elmes came to help people who were struggling to exist in the cold, bitter wind. Sand everywhere, and no shelter. How could I have forgotten?"

"So you already know about the Argelès camp?" said Pierre, surprised.

"Well, I had to research the work of Mary Elmes, and I found out that after she left Spain and went home to Ireland, she read about the terrible conditions in which the refugees were being held. She came here and did wonderful work helping the people on this beach. I had forgotten that this was the place that she had come to."

132 Pierre was impressed. "Well, of course, we all know about Mary Elmes — since she was awarded the honor of *Juste Parmi les Nations*, as it's called in French. But that was mainly about rescuing Jewish children. I didn't realize that she had worked here, too. You must tell me more! But first, I've got some news for you: Robert can take you to Rivesaltes the day after tomorrow. How does that fit in with your plans?"

"We don't have any plans really," said Dad. "That sounds fine to me. How do we meet him?"

"He thinks you should start as early as possible, as it gets very hot there this time of year. Could you be ready by 8:30? He will come here with his car, but you'll have to take your car as well. Is that okay?"

"Yes, okay," said Dad.

"Great, Wednesday morning then!" Turning to Emma he added, "If you would like to know more about what I was just talking about, I can show you if you've got a few minutes to spare."

"Do you mean all of us?" asked Emma.

"Well, whoever wants to come. It won't take long."

Mr. Collins said that he'd better stay, as Mum was still dozing in the shade and he didn't want to disturb her.

Andrew made some excuse about charging his camera, so it was just the two of them setting off together. Pierre led Emma through a side gate of the campsite and into a leafy lane that she hadn't seen before. They walked in silence at first, conscious of being alone together, neither of them wanting to be the first to break the spell.

Eventually Emma asked, "Where are we going?"

"Right here!" said Pierre, looking both ways before crossing the road. "Quick, while there are no cars coming."

On the opposite side of the road, a gate opened onto a small grassy square with a few trees. In the middle of the square there was a tall granite column containing lists of names on three of its sides. Next to it there was a smaller stone pillar with a bright shiny fairly new metal plaque containing three paragraphs, none of which were in English.

"What is this place?" asked Emma. "What does this plaque say?"

"This is a memorial," said Pierre. "The plaque is in three languages — Catalan, Spanish, and French. I'll translate it for you. It says, 'To the seventy children (less than ten years of age), Republicans, Catalans, Spanish, Jews, and Gypsies, who died in the camp of Argelès. We will always remember you and the story of your short lives.'"

Emma didn't know what to say. There were questions she wanted to ask, but at that moment it seemed right to keep silent. Pierre stood there looking at the memorial for a few moments. Then he said, "Look at the date," and pointed to the top of the writing.

Emma's eyes opened wide. She gasped. "In 2012? Only a few years ago! What happened in 2012?"

Pierre shook his head. "No, it wasn't a few years ago, it was 1939 and 1940. But that plaque is fairly new. It was only seven years ago, that it was placed here. See? There's an older one below it."

Indeed there was. It was a small yellow plaque with just a few words.

"I'll read it to you," said Pierre. "It says, 'The children's tree. Seventy children died in this camp. They were less than ten years old. This tree planted in 1999.'"

"Why are there two memorials saying the same thing?" asked Emma. "Well — almost the same thing."

"It took them sixty years to remember those children — many of them just babies. And even then, they didn't explain who they were. The newer plaque does at least tell a little more about them and promises that we will never forget. These children didn't die in the war in Spain. They died right here, in the camp that was supposed to give them shelter. They died of hunger, of disease, of the cold, and from lack of care. Hundreds of their parents died here, too. Look at the names on that column."

Emma stood looking at the memorial and then at Pierre. He must have been here many times; but she could see that it still made a great impression on him. They stood there together, under the trees, just the two of them, thinking of the seventy children.

Then Pierre turned and started walking towards the gates. "Let's go," he said. "There's something else you should see." They walked down the avenue and crossed the busy road running alongside the sea. Pierre walked onto the beach, followed by Emma.

"Look at all these people enjoying themselves. They come here to swim, sunbathe, and relax, and to enjoy the wonderful view of the Pyrenees. They've got no idea what happened here seventy-odd years ago! Did you know, there were *one hundred thousand* people — men, women, and children — crowded together on this beach? It was February, it was bitterly cold, and there was no shelter. Nothing at all! The men scraped holes in the sand to try to make some shelter. They were surrounded by barbed wire and the sea."

135

Of course, Emma had learned about the beach at Argelès. She turned to Pierre. "This really means something to you, doesn't it Pierre? Was your family here all those years ago?"

"Yes," he said. "Both my grandfathers and their families. They were all here. Most of the Spanish and Catalan folk living here today had parents or grandparents on this beach. Over two hundred of them died here."

He turned and began to walk back up to the road. Emma followed him.

"I read about this when I did some research for a presentation I had to give at school about Mary Elmes," said Emma. "Reading about it is one thing; but seeing the place and the cemetery for yourself is another thing altogether."

"Didn't they tell you about the Argelès Camp when you were on that tour bus?" asked Pierre.

"They didn't say anything at all," said Emma. "There wasn't any commentary about anything."

"That's what I mean," said Pierre. "Visitors are not told anything about the horrible things that happened here. It would be bad for tourism. It might give people nightmares. There are small plaques at each edge of the camp. You would never find them yourself. Someone who knew where they were would have to show them to you. But once you've heard what happened here, you can't visit this beach without thinking about it. They were Spanish immigrants, you see; and nobody wanted them here back then."

"But that plaque in the cemetery said that there were Jews and Gypsies as well. Where did they come from?"

"That was later," said Pierre. "That was after the war against Germany had started. By then, there were some barracks built on the beach. But conditions were still terrible. That was quite deliberate. The authorities wanted the Spanish to go home. They thought that if they made things too comfortable, they would just stay where they were."

"Just like the workhouses," said Emma.

Pierre was puzzled. "Workhouses?" he asked "What are those?"

"It was something we learned at school recently," said Emma. "When people had no work and were too poor to feed themselves, or when they needed medical treatment they couldn't afford, they would have to go to the workhouses. Married couples were separated, and they were made to do hard physical labor. Our teacher said that it was cruel, but the idea was that nobody would go to the workhouses unless they absolutely had to."

"That must have been a long time ago," suggested Pierre.

"No, not really. My Grandad said that he could remember people being terrified of the workhouses when he was a child. Thank goodness those days are over."

"Are they?" asked Pierre. "Don't you have immigrants and refugees in Ireland? We do, here in France."

"Well — yes. I suppose we do. But that's different, isn't it?"

"I don't think so," Pierre responded firmly. "The only real difference is that they arrive in ones and twos instead of half a million in just a few days."

137

Emma didn't reply. She didn't know what to say. She needed to think about it. People didn't die in Irish immigration centers, did they? But what happened to them when they were sent back to the countries they were trying to escape from?

Together they returned slowly to the campsite without saying much more to each other.

Then Pierre stopped at the gate and said, "Thanks for coming, Emma! Sorry if it was all a bit gloomy, but I thought you ought to know that Rivesaltes is not the only place around here where terrible things happened. And there were other camps like Argelès along the coast, at Saint-Cyprien and Le Barcarès, for example." He gave her a melancholy look as he touched her shoulder. "*À bientôt!*" he said.

She wanted to give him a hug, he looked so sad. But it could be misunderstood, she thought. So she just smiled back and said "*À bientôt.*"

CHAPTER SEVENTEEN
Collioure

That night, Emma stared at the ceiling for a long time. It wasn't that she couldn't get to sleep; it was just that there was so much to think about. She had come here to learn more about the camp where her grandfather lived as a baby, but now she had somehow stumbled onto another story altogether: a camp for Spanish refugees fleeing their bombed and battered homeland. Of course, she already knew some of this story from her work on Mary Elmes, but being here and seeing it for herself brought it to life. How extraordinary that this beautiful part of the world, which was never known for its battlefields or campaigns, could hide so many dreadful secrets of the past.

She was also thinking about Pierre. There was so much about him that she liked: the friendly, open way he chatted to everyone; his sense of humor; and his love of his ancestral homeland, Catalonia. The more she thought about it, the more she realized how little she actually knew about him. He had been very good at getting her to talk about herself, where she lived, what she liked to do, and above all of course, the reason why they were all here in Argelès. But what did she know about him? Did he have any brothers and sisters? What did his parents do? Come to think of it, he had never mentioned anything about his family at all, except that both his grandfathers had been in the camp at Argelès back in that bitter winter of 1939.

It was with these thoughts chasing through her mind, that Emma finally fell asleep.

It was Tuesday already! They were moving on to the next campsite on Saturday. That only left four days, and one of those would be taken up with the long-awaited visit to the Rivesaltes camp. At breakfast there was the usual discussion about what they would do today, and the usual disagreement about every idea proposed.

Mr. Collins thought it was too hot to do anything physically demanding and proposed lounging around the pool all day reading an Irish newspaper. His wife really wanted to go into Perpignan and have a good look at the shops, and perhaps drink a coffee, or even a glass of wine somewhere nice. Andrew was set on checking out the nearby Aqualand, a water park with a multitude of attractions — which included a couple of girls he had overheard planning such a trip yesterday.

And Emma? Well, Emma wanted to find out more about the Argelès Concentration Camp of seventy-odd years ago. What had it been really like? And why had it been allowed to happen? She felt that, armed with this knowledge, she might be able to get a little closer to

Pierre. Then she told herself that she should value knowledge for its own sake, and not as a means of impressing others.

In the end, the issue was settled when they all agreed to go their own separate ways. Andrew set off down the road to Aqualand. Emma walked in the opposite direction to find the tourist office where she hoped she might get more information, and Mr. Collins conceded and agreed to drive his wife the fifteen kilometers into Perpignan.

At the tourist office, Emma found several leaflets with information about the camp. There were some very graphic pictures showing a beach whose sand was totally invisible under a mass of human beings. There were soldiers in overcoats, old men in rags, children barefoot, women huddled in groups, and apart from some crude tents made from driftwood and canvas scraps, there appeared to be no shelter. It was very much as she had imagined it from Pierre's description. She wandered down to the beach, which although busy, still had vast areas of open sand. She realized just how many people there must have been here on that icy February night to completely cover the beach as it was in that picture.

Emma wandered slowly back to the campsite, her mind processing everything that she had read and seen.

There was nobody in their bungalow, which didn't surprise her. They wouldn't be back for hours yet. She took the brochures that she had picked up from the tourist office, and sat in the shade on their private deck.

She must have dozed off, she supposed, because she came to with a start as she heard her name spoken. It was Pierre, standing right outside the fence that surrounded their little garden.

"Sorry if I've disturbed you," he said with a smile.

141

She wondered how she must look, having been caught napping. "I was just resting my eyes," she said. "It's the sun. It's so bright!"

"You should try sunglasses," Pierre said, still grinning. "I just popped over from the bar. I'm working this morning, so I can't stay. Would you like to come out with me this afternoon to Collioure?"

Of course I would! But should I say so? "I'll have to ask my parents," she responded. "They might have planned something, I don't know. They're in Perpignan at the moment."

"Okay, I'll come back around 2:00. Will you know by then?"

"Maybe. What's this place you mentioned? They'll want to know where I'm going."

"Collioure. It's a beautiful fishing village. It's only a few minutes from here. You'll love it! Bring your camera. *À bientôt!*"

There was that grin again. He knew that she would say yes. And she knew that he knew!

Her parents were back soon after 1:00. Andrew hadn't returned; he would probably be gone all day. As they sat down to a quiet snack of cheese, baguettes, and white wine (diet coke for Emma), she thought carefully of how she was going to bring up the subject of going off with Pierre this afternoon. She was still anxiously turning the question over in her mind when he appeared.

He smiled at the family and said "*Bon appétit!*"

Mr. and Mrs. Collins were somewhat bemused by this and replied "*Bonjour!*" as that was the only greeting they were confident with.

Turning to Emma, Pierre asked, "So we're okay for Collioure then?"

Oh God, thought Emma. *Here we go!* Addressing her parents, she found herself saying in a voice she didn't recognize as her own, "Pierre invited me to go with him to a fishing village near here. Is that okay with you?"

"Where is this place? How are you going to get there?" demanded her father.

"It's Collioure, Mr. Collins!" replied Pierre. "We'll go on my scooter."

"Not with Emma on the back, you won't!" said her father sharply. "She's not going on any scooter with anybody! She hasn't got the gear for it, and that's *that!*"

Emma was mortified. She hadn't realized what Pierre was going to propose. If she had known, she would have told him that her parents would never agree to such an idea.

"Couldn't we go on the bus?" she asked Pierre.

"Yes," he replied somewhat unexpectedly. "There's quite a good bus service. Every hour or so. And it's only one euro each way."

Mr. Collins raised his eyebrows. This young man seemed to have an answer for everything. "How long will it take?" he asked.

Pierre assured him that the bus ride was no more than about twenty minutes, and that he promised to bring Emma back at a reasonable time.

"Well, what do you think of it?" asked Pierre.

They were sitting at the top of a short set of steps that climbed up from the path below and stretched along one of the stone walls of the *Château Royal*, lined with a canopy of olive trees providing welcome shade from the burning sun. In front of them, only a few feet below, was the harbor with the white sails of yachts fluttering in the breeze. Beyond the far side of the harbor, an ancient church rose up from the horizon, crowned with a dome that glowed in the sun.

"It's marvelous!" Emma said with a sigh. She had thought Argelès was pretty nice, but this was out of this world. "What a view!"

"Many famous artists used to come here to paint," said Pierre. "You can see why."

They had walked to the same bus stop where they had caught the train-bus the other day, and then they'd taken the ordinary bus to Collioure. The journey had been brief as Pierre had promised, but it had also been stunning. The road twisted and turned along the cliffs, providing views in all directions, sometimes of the bay past Argelès and Saint-Cyprien, and sometimes ahead to the foothills of the Pyrenees, tumbling into the deep blue waters of the Mediterranean.

"What would you like to do now?" asked Pierre.

"Can we just sit here for a while and enjoy the view?" pleaded Emma. "It's so hot out there, but there's a lovely breeze under these trees, and there's so much to take in."

So they sat there together as the world passed by below them. Kids were rushing about on their way in or out of the water, elderly folk strolled along, children played with buckets and spades, and couples walked hand in hand, oblivious of all else as they chattered and giggled. Emma had to pinch herself to be sure that it was really true — that she, Emma Collins, was sitting here in this paradise with a boy she had only known for three days. And what did she know of him? *Hardly anything, really.*

"You're quiet," said Pierre. "What are you thinking about?"

"Well, *you*, actually," replied Emma rather daringly. "I was just thinking that I don't know anything about you. You know all about why I'm here, the story about my grandad, and so on. I don't even know your last name!"

Pierre smiled. "There's not much to know, really. There's thousands of people like us in this part of France. We're the leftovers from the *Retirada* of seventy-five years ago."

"The *Retirada*? What's that?"

"That's the Catalan word for the great wave of refugees who left Spain to escape General Franco."

"But I still don't know anything about *you*!" exclaimed Emma. "Do you have brothers and sisters? Where do you live? What do your parents do? And what do you do when you're not working in the bar?"

"Okay, let's see. I have a sister, we live in Argelès, my Dad is a plumber, and I'm about to start my last year at *lycée* before going to university."

"And what are you going to study in college?"

"Well, I haven't quite decided yet. Not plumbing, at any rate! With my background, I feel that I would like to do something about refugees, but I'm not sure how to go about that. There's plenty of time still."

"And your grandparents — are they all still alive?"

"I think I told you that my two grandfathers were in the camps after the *Retirada*. They are both fine. So is my mom's mother. But Dad's mother, that's a bit complicated. Come to think of it, it's a bit like your family. My dad's mother died when he was born."

"So you only have one grandmother?" asked Emma.

"Well — my Grandad couldn't manage his work and look after my Dad when he was just a baby, so he got a young lady to help him, and not long afterwards they were married. So I have got two grandmothers, but only one of them is my biological grandmother."

"That must have been awful for your dad," said Emma. "Does he have any brothers or sisters?"

"He has two younger half-brothers, but he's not close with them. He's always felt somehow different, having a different mother I suppose."

Emma wondered whether this explained the strange kind of loneliness that she had noticed in Pierre. Was it because he was a Spanish boy brought up in France, and in a family that was broken by a death and remarriage? Was this the reason for his dwelling on the sad events of the beaches at Argelès?

"*Now* what are you thinking about?" teased Pierre.

"I was thinking that perhaps we should be moving along," she lied.

"Remember, you promised to get me back by 5:00!"

She got up quickly and started to descend the steep steps, but she misjudged both their height and length, and stumbled into the arms of Pierre who had anticipated her move. He held her for a moment, and then, taking hold of her hand, he said, "Here, let me help you down these steps. They're harder than they look!"

Not knowing what to say, she let him guide her down to the pathway, where, after a while he eventually let go of her hand. They walked on beneath the massive walls of the citadel, built hundreds of years ago to protect the harbor. Both of them were aware that something had just changed in their relationship, and neither of them dared to speak first.

Arriving at the bus stop, it appeared that there was nearly half an hour to wait for the next bus, so they sat at an outside table at a nearby café and ordered cold drinks. Somehow, the conversation seemed awkward, and when Emma eventually returned to the bungalow, she couldn't decide whether her first date with Pierre had been a success or a failure.

CHAPTER EIGHTEEN
Rivesaltes

It was Wednesday, the day of the visit to Rivesaltes — the camp where Grandad had lived as a baby. The family had an early breakfast, and was ready to go by 8:30, as planned. Right on time, Pierre arrived in a small car driven by a young man in his late twenties. They jumped out, and Pierre made the introductions.

"This is Mr. Duval, one of my teachers," he said. "He'll explain everything to you."

"Call me Robert," said the newcomer. "As Pierre said, I'm a teacher at his school. But I'm also a member of an activist group. We are mostly school teachers, although there are a few others among us. We are concerned that for years, children have been leaving school without the slightest knowledge of what happened around here back in the thirties and forties. We were afraid that if something wasn't done soon, there would be nobody left who remembered. And it's thanks to us and others like us that things are really happening at last. But enough talking! Let's get on our way. I suggest that Pierre goes with you in case we get separated, and one of you can come with me."

It was Andrew who jumped in beside Robert. Mr. and Mrs. Collins occupied the front of their own car, with Emma and Pierre in the back. Emma couldn't help thinking that this visit was off to a good start.

They made good progress along the fast two-lane highway towards Perpignan, but things slowed down somewhat as they passed through the city.

"There is a bypass," said Robert to Andrew, "but it isn't quite finished yet. And until it is, it's best to avoid it altogether."

They crossed the river and were soon in the suburbs. Over on the left they could see the airport, and soon after that, two rows of giant wind turbines made an appearance. In the second car, Pierre pointed these out to the family.

"This wind farm is built on part of the old internment camp," he said. "There's quite a large industrial site being built there, too. But there's still a large part of the old camp left just as it was seventy years ago."

They had turned off the highway now, and were weaving their way past newer buildings and through a series of roundabouts. They turned right at a sign pointing to the Memorial of the Rivesaltes Camp. A short distance later, the two cars pulled off the road onto a dirt path that was blocked by huge boulders. On the opposite side of the road, there was a series of commemorative monuments, each very different — some were rather imposing, some were quite crude, and all were looking the worse for wear.

They all got out, immediately aware of the heat of the sun. They stood in an immense plain, the mountains away to the west — the familiar outline of Canigou still visible, and away to the east across the plain, they could make out the blue of the Mediterranean.

They crossed the road to look at the monuments.

"Some of these have been here a long time; others are more recent," said Robert.

"Why are there so many?" asked Andrew.

"This camp has had many uses over the years, and all sorts of people have been detained here," explained Robert. "It started with the Spanish who were moved here when the camp at Argelès closed — I believe you know about that?" They all nodded and murmured agreement.

"Then there were the Jews — your relations among them. There were also Gypsies, Jehovah's Witnesses, political prisoners, and anybody the government took a dislike to. Later, when the fortunes of war swung the other way, German soldiers were imprisoned here. Finally, there were refugees from the war in Algeria. These monuments have been erected in memory of all these different people who suffered here. It was an awful place to be. You can feel the heat now, and it's still early. In the winter it can be icy cold. But worst of all was the wind — today it's not too bad! Now let's go and have a look at the camp. Careful how you cross the road." They walked back to where the cars were parked.

"A few years ago we would have walked down this path," said Robert. "But now that the Memorial Museum has been built, we have to drive around to the visitors' parking lot. They've placed these boulders here to stop people from wandering into the camp like they used to do."

They got back into their cars and drove off down the road. They were passing what was left of the camp on their right. They noticed the remains of old buildings, none of them having an intact roof, and few having much of their walls left. Only the concrete floors remained of most of them.

Pierre explained how Rivesaltes had come to replace Argelès as a home for the Spanish refugees.

"It was going to be so much better for them," he said. "There were proper buildings here, even outhouses and washing facilities. They had planned to have a hospital here, with trained staff always on hand. Everything was going to be organized with the welfare of the children in mind."

"So what went wrong?" asked Mr. Collins.

"Well, these things just never happened. Instead, more and more people were sent here, and eventually it became the assembly point for all the Jews living in the unoccupied zone. The overcrowding was terrible; there were rats and other vermin, diseases spreading throughout the camp, and people began to die in large numbers."

"Do you mean that it was like Auschwitz?" asked Mrs. Collins.

"No, nobody tried to kill people here. They just didn't try hard enough to keep them alive. So 215 people died here, including fifty-one children."

"Is there a cemetery here like the one Pierre showed me at Argelès?" asked Emma.

"No, they were all buried in the Rivesaltes town cemetery. There's a monument dedicated to them there."

"Can we find where Grandad must have lived?" asked Emma.

"No," replied Pierre. "You used to be able to go there, but now you can only go to the Museum and the area around it. *Îlot K* was where the Jews were confined. Originally, it was the area for the children, but when the camp was ordered to hold all the Jewish people for deportation to Drancy, *îlot K* became their prison. *Îlot* means 'little island.' Each *îlot* was surrounded by barbed wire, so they were prisons within the main prison."

They could see the parking lot just up ahead. It was big, with room for many cars and an area for coaches, too. But today, there were only about twenty cars or so sitting in the sunshine. They got out of their cars and followed Robert along the main path which led to an enormous rectangular depression in the ground.

"They decided to build the Memorial Museum below ground," explained Robert. "They wanted visitors to experience the vastness of the original camp, but that would have been ruined by constructing a big new building on the surface. So it was built in this huge hole in the ground, with only the top showing. We can go down that ramp into the museum, but first let's walk around the perimeter where there is much to see."

There was a concrete walkway surrounding the building on all four sides, and the six of them walked around it slowly, passing the ruins of barracks and latrines. At intervals there were notices explaining various remains. The view of the former camp stretched out before them on an immense plain. It was desperately ugly and monotonous, devoid of any attraction whatsoever. Yet in the far distance, there was a glimpse of another world. The magnificent majesty of Canigou rose high above the horizon, not yet snow-capped as it is in winter, but incredibly beautiful — reminding those who saw it that there was still a natural beauty to creation that even this man-made horror could not obliterate.

Emma turned to Pierre, knowing that he loved this mountain. "How high is it?" she asked.

"Canigou?" said Pierre. "I'm not sure exactly, but I think that it's just under 3000 meters."

"The highest mountain in Ireland is just over 1000," said Mr. Collins. "So this one is nearly three times as high."

They turned to begin the long descent down the ramp, and eventually reached the museum entrance. They paid for admission and bought a guidebook, then continued along a corridor before coming out into a vast hall. All around them on the walls were pictures and videos. They were divided into different sections, each showing a different stage in the history of the camp.

"This was the largest internment camp in Western Europe," explained Robert. "And probably the longest lasting, too. It held prisoners from 1941 to 1977, and at one time had the second-largest population in the Pyrenees *Orientales*, exceeded only by the city of Perpignan."

The group split up and spent another hour or so wandering around, watching videos, looking at pictures, and examining the many artifacts displayed under glass in the center of the hall. Unfortunately there was not much to read that was in English, but the pictures spoke for themselves.

"Isn't it incredible to think that Grandad was here?" whispered Emma to her brother.

"Yes, and even more incredible that he was rescued by an Irish lady, only to end up in Ireland himself!"

"Of course, I'd forgotten that," said Emma. "We'll have so much to tell him!"

They eventually left the museum after buying some pictures and an English version of the guidebook. They walked slowly back to the parking lot.

"I've got one more thing to show you before we leave Rivesaltes," said Robert. "Hop in the cars and follow me. Stay close behind. Try not to let another car get between us."

They drove back down the way they had come and reached a roundabout in the industrial area where there was a car factory. Robert's car led the way past hundreds of brand-new vehicles parked and ready for delivery all over France. Then he turned into a pleasant, tree-lined road flanked by recently built houses. They parked and got out.

155

"This was all part of the camp originally," explained Robert. "Now have a look at this." He pointed to a long straight stony stretch similar to the track they had seen earlier. "See how this track bends to the left down there? See that line of trees that follows the bend? This used to be the railway track. It curved around to the left, and just beyond where you can see the freeway it joined the main line. The freeway wasn't there back then of course." He bent down. "Look, you can see where the sleepers were fixed to the ground here and here." He pointed to marks in the track. "And look — here is one of the coupling bolts that held the railway line to the sleepers. This, Mr. Collins, is where your aunt boarded the train that took her and thousands of others to their deaths in Poland. But when the first convoys left, there was no railway here yet. They left from the railway station in the town of Rivesaltes. But the passengers taking the train to Perpignan or Narbonne were horrified to see hundreds of people in filthy clothes being pushed into cattle wagons. There were even people attempting suicide. So the authorities quickly decided to build a line into the camp, and spare the good citizens of France from the sight of such awful scenes!

They just stood there, silently viewing the scene and thinking.

Eventually Robert broke the silence. "All these years," he said, "this place has just been left to crumble away. No one has bothered to protect what is, after all, an archeological site of historical importance. It's only recently that those boulders were put in to stop people from driving in and taking away whatever they could find. That's why we formed our little group: to campaign for a decent memorial museum on this site. And at last, we have been successful, and now this place will never be forgotten."

Andrew had a question for Robert that he had wanted to ask for some time. "Was Rivesaltes a concentration camp? Is that the right word to use? I noticed that you and Pierre both called it an 'internment camp.' Could you explain the difference?"

"That's a very good question, and a very difficult one to answer," replied Robert. "When it was first opened to take in the Spanish folk from Argelès, it was called a center of *hébergement*. That means 'accommodation.' You would use that word if you were looking for a hotel or a bed and breakfast. It certainly wasn't the appropriate word to use here. You could say that it was a concentration camp, because people were packed in together here against their will in order to be sent elsewhere. It was easier to do that if they were concentrated in one place. But since that word has come to be associated with the death camps like Auschwitz, maybe 'internment' is a better word. The important thing, though, is not what word is used. What's much more important is to know and remember what happened here, and to make sure that nothing like it could ever happen again."

The little party stood there, silent and thoughtful until Robert spoke again. "Well, now I suggest that we go and find somewhere cool to eat some lunch, and if you have any other questions, I will do my best to answer them. Let's go!"

They found a bistro not too far away, and were comfortably seated in the shade when Robert said, "I've just thought of something! Have you made any plans for tomorrow?"

"Well, no," Mr. Collins answered. "Nothing special. I suppose we should think about all that we have discovered, probably make some notes, and above all, we should write to Grandad and tell him what we've found out. Did you have something in mind?"

"Yes, I do believe there's something else you should see. If you've got the time, say a couple of hours, I could take you somewhere that you'll certainly find interesting. And you might just possibly learn something more about your father."

Mr. Collins looked at the others. "You okay for some more discoveries?" he asked.

They all agreed.

"I'll be around at about 10:00 then, if thats' okay?" asked Robert as he got up to leave.

"Okay!" said Mr. Collins.

"*À bientôt!*" called Emma.

CHAPTER NINETEEN
Margaret

April 1942

Mary Elmes leaned over the balcony of her third-floor apartment and gazed down at the street. It was still early, but the sun was up and the day promised to be fine. The trees on the Avenue des Baléares were already covered in leaves and would provide shade from the heat later in the summer. But even on this April day it was warm and there was a gentle breeze. It will not be this nice where I am going later today, *she thought grimly.*

She had a visitor staying with her for a couple of days. Margaret Smith from the head office in Philadelphia in America was over on a fact-finding trip. She had recently arrived in France and was based out of its main office in Marseille for the most part. But at her own request, she was now traveling around the various Quaker depots, seeing for herself what the conditions were really like. Today, Mary was going to take her visitor to the nearby camp of Rivesaltes, where over 3000 men, women, and children were being detained in appalling conditions. She wondered how this elegantly dressed woman from the still peaceful United States of America would react when confronted with the harsh realities of life in one of the many concentration camps of southern France.

They breakfasted together rather less lightly than Mary was accustomed to, spent time discussing some of the problems that were troubling them, and then around noon they set off for the camp in the little Ford driven by Mary's chauffeur, Victor. Like over half of the inmates in the camp they were visiting, Victor was Spanish.

Margaret watched the passing scenes through the car's windows. Although Perpignan suffered badly from all kinds of shortages, the city hadn't been damaged by military action. At a quick glance, it looked almost pleasant. Only the drab and shabby clothes worn by the pedestrians and the empty storefronts along the once-booming Boulevard des Pyrénées suggested any suffering by the city's inhabitants. In truth, everybody was hungry — very hungry. But none more so than the inmates of the camp where they were headed.

Soon, they were crossing the river Tet and driving through farmland. The fields were badly tended though — many of the workers still being held prisoner in German war camps, two years after the armistice. It was flat now, and Margaret noticed that it seemed windier here than in the city. They turned to the right and passed through what used to be grassy meadows, but now this plain was covered only in dust and stones, and with the dust being swept up by the wind, visibility was quite poor.

They passed between two large concrete pillars and came to a halt alongside a low brick building. A guard examined their papers and waved them through. Evidently they are well-known here, thought Margaret.

"We'll get out here and walk," announced Mary. "Hold on to your hat or you might lose it!" And indeed, it was extremely windy. Margaret looked

around. The view of barrenness would have stretched as far as her eyes could see, but it was interrupted by row upon row of single-story concrete barracks. They were widely spaced and could have seemed decent if set in grassland and separated by flower beds. But there was nothing but dust and stones. Margaret thought that she had never seen so many stones. Not a blade of grass could be found, not even a weed. It was a desert of dust.

They made their way between the barracks, heads down and eyes almost shut to keep out the dust. The heat was oppressive too, the sun's glare causing them to seek some shade, but in vain as there was none.

"Where is everybody?" asked Margaret, for there was nobody to be seen.

"They all stay in their barracks when the tramontane *is blowing," said Mary. "And that's most of the time. In the summer it's a scorching blast, and in the winter it's icy cold. And there's no escaping it. The dust gets into your clothes, your bed, even your food. This is a terrible place to be. It was originally built as an army camp, but abandoned because it was deemed unfit for the horses. Now over 700 children call it home."*

161

"What are those taller buildings with stairs outside?" asked the American visitor.

"They are the latrines. They are open to the skies, with just a hole in the floor and a bucket underneath!"

Margaret shook her head in disbelief. "And you said that there are mothers with babies here?"

"Oh yes! Many of the women were pregnant when they were rounded up and brought here. Death among the babies is common. We hope to take some women out of here for a break while they give birth if we can arrange it."

"And then they will have to bring their newborn children back to this?" *asked Margaret in horror, looking around at the desolation.*

"I'm afraid so. Mothers who have been in other camps tell me that this is the worst one of all because of the wind." She led the way around one of the buildings. "Here we are at the dining hall."

The dining hall was a concrete barrack, just like all the others. But stretching down the side of the building were several lines of children, each holding a tin can in their hands. Many of them were barefoot, though some had sandals that appeared to have been made from old car tires. They were all ill-clad and stood there patiently, with silent, scrunched-up faces, buffeted by the wind howling between the barracks.

The two women entered through a doorway that was adorned with bright paintings of a train, a truck, an airplane, and a ship.

Mary pointed out the ship, which had America's stars and stripes on its side. "That's supposed to be a Quaker ship bringing supplies from America," she explained. "But the ship seldom comes because of the British blockade."

"British blockade?" asked Margaret.

"Yes. The British have imposed a total blockade on all French ports, to cut supplies to the German troops. But of course it also means great hardship for French civilians, and the people in the camps are the last to get anything that does come through. Technically, they are supposed to get a daily ration, which is just enough to stay alive. But it passes through various hands on its way through the camp system, and each pair of hands takes a cut. So by the time it reaches its intended recipient, there's very little left. Fortunately, the children receive supplementary rations from organizations like ours that are imported from across Europe, but there's nothing extra for the adults — and that includes the teenagers."

By now the children were filing into the room and showing their cards to one of the helpers, then proceeding to the table where their crude containers were filled from a steaming pot of rice and milk. Each child watched the big ladle filling their can with great concentration, and if a little dribbled down the side, they immediately licked it up so as not to lose even one grain of rice. They then sat down on the benches, pulled spoons from their pockets and devoured the food as quickly as possible.

"I have watched many children eat their dinner," said Margaret quietly to her companion. "Usually there is talking and laughter — often too much — and they have to be told to behave. But look at these children — there isn't a sound except for the scraping of their spoons in the tin cans. Look at their little faces as they devour the last scraps of rice!"

Later, the two women were in another barrack which had been converted into a workshop, where several female prisoners were making shoes. A teacher working in the camp came in and was introduced to the American visitor.

"When we gave these children paper and crayons and let them draw what they liked," said Mercedes, the teacher, "most of them just drew pictures of barracks. They were born in the camps, and had never seen anything else. They knew nothing of houses, shops, streets full of people — nothing at all of the outside world. What sort of adults will these half-starved, captive children grow up to be? And when we decorated their dining hall with a colorful border of green fields and rabbits, the children were terrified because they thought they were rats. Rats are the only creatures they know."

The three women moved out into the open air. The wind had died down. If there were any shade it could have been almost pleasant. Some of the less sick men and women began to appear in the spaces between the barracks. But there was nowhere for anyone to sit — no chairs, no benches, no grassy banks, nothing but the rocky, dusty ground. Some did sit down among the stones, and had great difficulty getting up again. Mary Elmes and her visitor moved among them, and they were frequently being stopped by people who wished to have a few words with the Irish worker. Margaret Smith noticed how they seemed to value the words that 'Miss Mary' (as they called her) had to say as she listened patiently to their problems and requests.

"*It's not just us!*" *Mary told Margaret in the car on the way back to Perpignan.* "*The Swiss Red Cross does a wonderful job here, too, as does the OSE, the Jewish Children's Aid Service. We all do everything we can, but it's nothing more than a drop in the ocean.*"

164

CHAPTER TWENTY
The Maternity at Elne

Robert was as good as his word, promptly arriving at 10:00 a.m. "We can cram into this old car if you want," he said. "But we'd probably be more comfortable in yours, if you don't mind driving again."

Emma looked around for Pierre, but there was no sign of him.

Robert noticed her uncertainty and said, "If you're looking for Pierre, I'm afraid he can't join us today. He's needed at home, apparently."

Emma had just assumed that he would be coming as well, as nothing had been said yesterday to suggest otherwise. On the other hand, he hadn't said that he would be coming, so perhaps she should have invited him. And there were only two days left. If she wanted to get to know him better, she couldn't afford to miss any opportunities. *Is this engagement at home just an excuse?*

Emma became aware that they were all getting into her dad's car.

"Daydreaming again!" chided her mother. "Come on! Robert hasn't got all day."

"Where are we going?" asked Mr. Collins, fastening his seat belt.

"Just down the road, really," answered the teacher. "We're going to a place called the *Château d'en Bardou*. It's not what you would call a castle in Ireland, it's more like a big house. But it's beautiful. And it's got a remarkable history that you may find very interesting."

"Which way do I go?" asked Mr. Collins, pulling out through the campsite gate.

"You know the way out onto the main road. When you get there, turn right towards Elne and Perpignan — the way we went to Rivesaltes yesterday."

It took only a few minutes to reach the turn for Elne. Emma was gazing out of the window, but not really taking in what her eyes were seeing. She didn't notice the magnificent cathedral as they crawled past it in the heavy traffic, nor was she aware that they were soon out in the country again, and passing beneath the railway line.

"Turn right here!" ordered Robert.

They were driving down a narrow lane, and just ahead through the trees Emma could see a most remarkable building. It was square in shape, not very big, but unusually tall, and the top was crowned with a large glass dome.

"You have to park around here, in the field," said Robert to Mr. Collins. "If you're lucky, you may be able to find some shade along this wall."

A few minutes later, they all jumped out of the car and followed another family walking towards the entrance gate.

"What is this place, Robert?" asked Mrs. Collins.

"As I mentioned, it's called the *Château d'en Bardou*, but most people know it as the Swiss Maternity. You will be able to pick up some leaflets about it once we're inside, but I'll give you a few details now while we walk. A young woman from the Swiss Red Cross came here in 1939. She realized that this building — which was empty and deserted — would make a fine hospital where she could bring pregnant women from the camp at Argelès, somewhere where they could give birth in peace and safety. Her name was Elisabeth Eidenbenz. When the refugees were moved to Rivesaltes, she carried on her work there, too — and Jewish women as well as Spanish women had their babies here. When the deportations commenced, she helped hide Jewish children here."

167

They were at the entrance. "There's a small fee for entry," said Robert. "It goes towards the upkeep of this place. It was only a few years ago that this house was rediscovered nearly in ruins, and it's been an expensive business getting it into shape again."

Inside the building, they found themselves looking at panels explaining the events of 1939 and onwards. There were pictures of the mothers and their children, and some of the pictures were really shocking, showing babies who were nothing but skin and bone.

Robert stepped forward and caught their attention. "That was really dreadful," he said. "But look here. In this place the mothers were fed properly. They had the kind of care that you would expect to find in a peacetime hospital. It was a wonderful break for them. But of course they had to go back eventually, to make room for others."

"How many babies were born here?" asked Mrs. Collins.

"About 600. If we go upstairs, you can see all their names."

So upstairs they went, and there, hanging from the ceiling, was a huge list of names. It reached from the ceiling to the floor, and in four columns it listed every child born in this house, from the first, in December 1939, to the last, in April 1944.

"Why are only the first names shown, with just an initial for the last names?" Emma asked a guide who was seated at a table full of leaflets.

"Because many are still alive, and we must respect their privacy," she replied.

168   Emma was looking down the lists. They were ordered by date. She came to the date of her grandfather's birth, February 13th, 1942, and there it was: *Franz K!*

For a moment, she couldn't speak. Then she gasped. "Look! Look! It's Grandad! He must have been one of those born here, too!"

The others looked where she was pointing. "It's the right date, sure enough," said Father. "It's got to be him. What do you think, Robert?"

"It would be quite a coincidence if it were *not* your father!" he replied. "Everything matches. You know that your grandparents were in the camp of Rivesaltes. So I would say that this is where he was born. I was hoping that we might be lucky and find him on this list. I'm so glad I thought of bringing all of you here!"

There were two more floors to explore, all filled with panels containing photographs of the mothers and their babies.

"Perhaps your father and his mother are here," said Mrs. Collins to her husband.

Unfortunately none of the pictures had names or other details, so the family couldn't identify anybody.

"After all the terrible things we've seen in Paris, Argelès and Rivesaltes, it's wonderful to find this place where everything was clean and welcoming, and where they must have felt safe — if only for a short time," said Mrs. Collins.

"Yes. But it wasn't as safe as you might think," said Robert. "Elisabeth was supposed to tell the authorities if any Jewish mothers or babies were here. But of course, she didn't. Their names were changed and they were passed off as Spanish. But one day, a German officer came and took away a Jewish mother for deportation while Elisabeth just stood there helplessly, unable to save her. Elisabeth was arrested by the Gestapo eventually. But she was released, as they could prove nothing against her, and she had the protection of her Swiss neutrality."

169

They were back at the campsite by lunchtime.

Emma wandered over to the bar to see if Pierre was there, but there was no sign of him. She joined the rest of her family at the pool for the afternoon. They had much to talk about, and they were looking forward to their departure on Saturday with mixed feelings. Mr. Collins was keen to get to their campsite in Provence, which had been his first-choice destination until the business of Rivesaltes and Grandad had cropped up. Andrew and Mother were quite happy where they were, and didn't particularly want to leave.

And Emma — well, Emma couldn't even bear to think of moving on and perhaps never seeing Pierre again! But she was thrilled that they had learned another fact about her grandfather, and she looked forward to sharing all of this with him when they returned home. How she wished that Pierre had been there, too, to share her excitement.

CHAPTER TWENTY ONE
Saying Good-bye

It was Friday, and not much had been planned for the day. It was to be a quiet day, and the last bit of packing could wait until tomorrow morning. Andrew had persuaded his father to join him on a last visit to Aqualand, the water park he had visited alone earlier in the week. As usual, Mother had plenty to keep her busy in and around the bungalow, although she was also hoping to find time to relax before tomorrow's journey. She would have to do her share of the driving, after all.

That left Emma on her own with no real idea of how to spend her time. Of course, she could have gone to Aqualand with Dad and Andrew, but she didn't want to miss Pierre in case he turned up unexpectedly. Having nothing better to do, she turned on her iPhone. She saw that her friends had posted some pictures of their summer adventures in other parts of the world. The gossip and rumors about John Braddock and her seemed to have died down, she noticed. She wondered where he was at the moment. What sort of holiday was he having? Was he all on his own? He couldn't possibly be any lonelier than she was feeling right now.

"Hi! *Ça va?*"

Pierre! Right there, on the other side of the fence. "*Ça va,*" she answered. She wasn't sure what it meant, but she knew by now that it was what you were supposed to say. She supposed it was like saying hello.

"What are you up to?" asked Pierre.

"Nothing much. How about you?"

He shrugged. "This and that. Want to come have a drink?"

She wondered if she should try not to appear too eager. But with only one day left, that might be fatal. "Okay, I'll just tell Mum where I'm going."

They walked over to the bar. One of the other guys there said something to Pierre and laughed. Pierre didn't seem to be amused, and ignored him.

"What would you like?"

"Can I have an ice cream?" asked Emma.

"What flavor?"

"Strawberry, please."

"Get us a table. I'll bring it over."

As Emma walked to a table in the shade, she heard him say something to the girl behind the bar and there was another burst of laughter. She felt uncomfortable, guessing they were talking about her, but she wasn't sure what was going on.

Pierre returned with ice cream for both of them.

They sat, eating their ice cream and saying nothing.

This is stupid! thought Emma. *Why aren't we talking?* So she decided to take the initiative. "Tomorrow, we're off," she said.

173

"I know."

"Is that all you have to say?" she asked, irritated.

"What else is there to say?" asked Pierre.

"Well, you could say that you're sad we're leaving!"

"Of course I'm sad!" said Pierre. "It's been great meeting you. But all good things must come to an end, don't they?"

"Does there have to be an end? Can't we keep in touch?"

"We can try, but my guess is that it won't last long. We've both got our lives to lead. There's school, friends, family, and all sorts of other stuff. When you're hundreds of kilometers apart, there's not much to say."

Emma was shocked. She couldn't understand how Pierre could talk like this. Surely he liked her? Hadn't they got on well? When he held her hand the other day after she had nearly fallen, he hadn't been in a hurry to let go. She didn't know what to say.

Pierre looked at her. He could see she was upset and puzzled. "I'm sorry!" he said. "I didn't mean to be rude. But it's true, isn't it? We've got on well together, but now it's time to go, and that's that. It's been great knowing you, and I wish you were staying longer, but you're not. So we have to say good-bye!

"Not *à bientôt* this time?" she asked quietly.

He smiled. "Not *à bientôt* this time, I'm afraid. That means 'see you soon,' and we won't be seeing each other soon — probably not ever!"

"But you said you wanted to go to England to improve your English," she said.

"Yes, well maybe there's a chance we might meet up. But England's not Ireland is it? And who knows what might happen by then, anyway?"

There was a shout from the bar, and more laughter.

Pierre stood up. He took Emma's hand in his own. "Look," he said. "I'll do what I can to try and find out about your Grandad's sister. If I find anything, I'll let you know. So maybe you will hear from me — it's possible. But right now, I've got to go. I'm on duty for the rest of the day. I'm sorry. Take care!" He gave her hand a squeeze, and then he was gone.

Emma walked slowly back to the bungalow. Her mother was hanging out some laundry.

"Did you see him? Was he there?"

"Who?" said Emma, knowing full well who Mother was talking about.

"Pierre, of course! That's who you've been mooning over for the last day or two, isn't it?"

"I don't moon over people!" said Emma, crossly. "Yes, he was there. But now, he's gone!"

"You're rather fond of him, aren't you?" asked her mother.

This was the last thing Emma wanted right now — to be interrogated about her feelings for Pierre.

"No," she said.

Mrs. Collins raised her eyebrows. "Really? You could have fooled me."

"Well, if you think you know everything about me, why do you ask?" snapped Emma, thoroughly annoyed.

Her mother didn't answer. *This needs to be handled carefully*, she thought to herself. "Can you give me a hand hanging these things out?" she asked.

Emma looked at the pile of washing and nodded.

Being rather traditional, her mother thought about how helpful Emma had always been around the house. *She'll make a good wife some day.* Aloud she said, "You can always twitter him."

Emma rolled her eyes in despair. "You don't twitter people, Mother! You tweet them! But anyway, he says there's no point. He says we'll only keep it up for a while, and then it'll all go dead."

"He's probably right," said her mother. "Summer romances are notoriously short-lived. What seems so wonderful in a strange place under a burning sun can seem unreal when you're back at home in rainy Ireland."

Emma managed a faint smile. "It wasn't really like that, Mum. I'm not just some silly teenager with a crush on some foreign lad. He was different. It's hard to explain, but I really felt there was something special between us. We seemed to have so much in common. He felt it, too, I'm sure. It was as if we'd met before in some other life or something. I just can't believe that I'll never see him again!"

Mrs. Collins put down the towel she was about to hang up, and put her arm around her daughter. "Do you know what I think?" she asked. "If something is really meant to be — then it will be. I really believe that."

Emma shook her head silently. Then she gave her mother a kiss. Finally, she said, "Thanks for understanding."

CHAPTER TWENTY TWO
À bientôt, Emma!

It was their final day in Argelès. Mr. and Mrs. Collins had spent the morning packing up, while Emma and Andrew went back and forth dealing with trash, water, and other necessities. Emma was watching out for some sign of Pierre, but all in vain. At last the car was crammed with their belongings, the bills were paid, and they set off through the gate on their way to the next campsite in Nice, the next destination of their journey.

Andrew was riding in the front seat next to his father, while his mother and sister shared the back seat. It was a fairly silent family that saw the now familiar outline of Canigou falling behind them as they sped north.

There was so much to think about, and not a lot to say. They had already discussed all that they had discovered about Grandad's origins, and what still remained a mystery. They knew the name of Grandad's father, but they didn't know what had become of him after he was transferred from Rivesaltes to some unknown labor camp. They knew that his mother was transported to Auschwitz and almost certainly died there. They also knew that Grandad had a sister named Lotte, and that she had somehow survived the moves and was taken to the *Château de Larade*, a Spanish children's colony in Toulouse. But there, the trail ran cold, and it seemed that they would never know what became of her. They knew that Grandad had been born in the comfort of the Swiss Maternity in Elne — they had discovered that just the other day. And finally, they had learned that it was Mary Elmes, the Irish lady awarded the Righteous Among the Nations medal by Yad Vashem in Jerusalem, who had rescued Grandad and his sister.

Emma was thinking about what they'd learned too, but she had other things on her mind. Naturally, she was thinking about Pierre. *Will we keep in touch? Will I ever see him again?* How could he just say good-bye to her in such a casual manner? Perhaps he was feeling just as devastated as she was, but didn't want to show it. That made her think of her great-grandmother, Helga Krauch. How could she just let her children go like that? She had struggled with it, hadn't she? But she had done what she thought was right in the end.

And Mother was right, of course; the time Emma had spent with Pierre could be counted in hours — almost in minutes. It hardly seemed possible that only last week they had not even met. What chance did such a brief relationship stand? She was thinking too about how she had changed over the course of the last few days. How her attitudes had been altered as she became aware of what made people different from each other, and how little these differences mattered. It didn't matter whether someone was an only child, was left-handed, had red hair, or didn't use WhatsApp. Those differences were nothing compared to being a refugee, a Jew in 1940s France, a Gypsy, or just someone the government decided it didn't like. Yet differences could all cause loneliness and misery. She remembered reading about a girl who killed herself because she was bullied on social media. She would certainly think again before making hasty judgements about immigrants and any other less fortunate people. Suddenly, it occurred to her for the first time that she, too, was from an immigrant family. She owed her very existence to Mary Elmes and people like her. She thought of John Braddock and how unpopular he was, and how she was ridiculed because she'd been seen with him.

Yes, she had changed — and she believed it was for the better.

They were passing lagoons full of flamingos when Emma's iPhone buzzed. To her delight, she saw that it was a text from Pierre. It read: *We think we may have found your Grandad's sister! Please call me!*

"You've got to stop the car, Dad!" she yelled from the back seat. "It's important!"

"I can't just stop on the freeway," her father answered, half turning his head towards her. "Is something wrong? If it's important I'll pull in at the next service area."

"No, it's good news, I think. But I've got to call Pierre."

Her call was answered right away. Emma didn't waste time on small talk. "Where did you find her?" she asked excitedly. "Is she all right? How old is she?"

"Can you come back? Now? I'll explain everything then," Pierre said.

Emma looked out the window. They were slowing down and turning off the freeway. "I'll call you back in a minute," she answered.

Her father parked the car in a shady spot under some trees, some distance from the service area buildings. "Now, what's this all about?" he demanded.

"I'm not sure," said Emma. "Pierre says that they may have found Grandad's sister, and he asked if we could go back immediately. I'm going to call him back now and find out more."

The family got out of the car and found places to sit while Emma made her call.

"Look — we're not certain, that's why we need you to come back. There's something you need to see, to confirm. But if it is her, I'm afraid she isn't still alive. She died a few years ago," said Pierre.

Emma, still shocked by this turn of events, said, "Can you explain all this to my dad? He won't want to turn back unless he knows exactly what's going on." With that, she handed the phone to her father.

"Hello Pierre," he said. "This is Emma's dad. She says that you have some important news for us?"

"Hello Mr. Collins! Yes, it is very important, I think! We believe we have found out what happened to your aunt, and we can introduce you to her son. He would very much like to meet you if it's not too late!"

"Well, we're about an hour down the road, but I suppose in these circumstances we ought to turn back! Where shall we meet you?"

"Will you be coming down the main road from Perpignan?" asked Pierre.

"Yes, down the D914."

"When you turn off for Argelès, there's a shopping center. We'll be right outside McDonald's."

"Right — see you in about an hour. Bye!"

Mr. Collins handed the phone back to Emma. "Well this is a shake-up!" Dad explained. "If he's right, he may have Grandad's sister's son with him, and he wants to meet us. That would be my cousin! How on earth has all this come about?"

The traffic was heavy going through Perpignan, and it was over an hour and a half before they pulled up outside the McDonald's.

"They're over there!" cried Emma, pointing to a car parked across the lot.

"I'll drive over," said her father, restarting the engine. He reversed, and then cruised over to park alongside the Citroën. Pierre and a middle-aged gentleman rose from the picnic table where they were seated and came to greet them.

"Thanks for coming back, Mr. Collins," said Pierre. "This is Carlos Sanchez. He has something he wants to show you."

Señor Sanchez stepped forward and seized Mr. Collins' hand, which he shook enthusiastically. He was speaking in rapid Spanish — or was it Catalan? — and of course nobody in the Collins family could understand a word he said.

"I'm afraid he doesn't speak any English, so I'll have to translate for you," said Pierre. He turned to Mr. Sanchez and said something to him. Mr. Sanchez nodded and smiled broadly. "He believes that his mother may be your aunt," Pierre said, addressing Emma's father. "He has something here he wants to show to you."

Mr. Sanchez then opened his wallet, took something out, and handed it to Mr. Collins. It was an old faded photograph — or more specifically, part of an old faded photograph, because it had been roughly torn in half.

Emma, peering over her father's shoulder, cried, "It's the other half of Grandad's photo! Turn it over and see what's written on the back, Dad!"

Mr. Collins obediently turned the photo over. "There's nothing there," he reported. "It's blank." Then turning to Mr. Sanchez he asked, "Where did you find this?"

Pierre answered for him. "It belongs to his uncle." Then addressing Emma he asked, "Are you sure that it's the same picture as the one that you told me about?"

Before she could answer, Andrew interrupted. "Have you got Grandad's photo with you, Emma?"

"No, but I've got the copy of what you made on the computer when you enhanced the writing on the back." She ran to the car and returned a minute or so later with it in her hands. The others crowded around her.

"But this is only a scan of the writing. And it's the wrong side of the picture. So we can't be certain that it's the same photo," complained Andrew.

His father took the printout from him and held it up to the light. "Look," he said. "See the torn edge? You can see where the picture was torn on its right side. Now look at Mr. Sanchez's picture. It's torn on the left — and the tears match perfectly! See that jagged bit at the top? It's the same on both, too!"

Then Andrew took the picture. "And I remember Grandad's picture had just a part of someone else sitting by the door of the house, and the rest was torn off. Well, look here! There's the rest of that person; she's holding a baby in her arms."

Mr. Collins turned to Pierre, his eyes welling up. "This *is* the same picture," he said, simply. "Now, tell us what all this means. Who is this gentleman, and how is he connected to my Aunt Lotte? Let's go sit down somewhere and hear all about it over some drinks."

They decided that this called for something a bit more exciting than coffee in a plastic cup, so they all trooped through the parking lot to a nearby bistro, where they ordered a bottle of local wine for the adults and cokes for the youngsters.

"This is going to be a bit complicated," Pierre said with a strange smile on his face. "I'll try to keep it as simple as I can. Mr. Sanchez here never knew his mother. She died giving birth to him. His father couldn't manage a baby on his own, so he remarried rather quickly."

At this point, Pierre glanced at Emma who was staring at him in amazement.

He continued, "His father moved into a new house to start over again with his new wife, and he gave all of his dead wife's personal belongings to one of his brothers. This upset his family; they thought it was disrespectful to his dead wife, so he drifted away from them. As a result, Mr. Sanchez grew up not knowing anything at all about his birth mother. Not that the rest of his family knew much, either. They had always assumed that she was one of those Spanish women of the *Retirada*, an orphan without any background. Mr. Sanchez knew that his uncle — his father's brother — had kept the few things that his mother had possessed. I told him about your picture, and he said he had seen something similar in a box at his uncle's house when he was a boy. So yesterday he went to see his uncle and asked if he could have a look at the box. And there was this picture!"

He turned to Mr. Collins. "Are you sure that this is part of the same picture?" he asked.

"Absolutely!" said Emma's father. "There's no doubt about it. My grandmother must have kept this half of the picture and given it to her little girl when they parted ways. What a miracle that it has survived! I suppose the people who took her in and looked after her realized its importance. So Mr. Sanchez's mother was Lotte, my aunt, and Mr. Sanchez is my cousin!" He turned to the Spaniard who was standing there smiling and grasped him by the hand. "If only I could speak Spanish!"

While all this was going on and the rest of the family hung on to every word, Emma just sat there, her drink in her hand, her jaw dropped in astonishment. Her eyes were fixed on Pierre as he was talking, but he carefully avoided her gaze. Then, when everybody had settled down, he turned to Emma with a broad smile on his face.

"I think Emma has worked out that I've been holding something back," he said. "Go on, you tell them!"

All eyes now turned to Emma.

Mrs. Collins' hand went to her mouth. *Oh my God,* she thought, *he's asked her to marry him!* But she was both relieved and astonished when her daughter finally spoke.

Emma blurted out, "I think that Pierre knows Mr. Sanchez rather better than he's let on. I think that Pierre's full name is Pierre Sanchez, and that this gentleman is his father. So Pierre's related to us too!"

Amid the gasps of surprise and smiles of pleasure, Pierre strode across to Emma and gave her a great big hug. "We're second cousins, Emma!"

But Mrs. Collins was still puzzled. "I don't get it," she said.

Emma turned to her. "Grandad and Pierre's grandma were brother and sister. They were both together at the Rivesaltes camp! Didn't I tell you that there was something different about Pierre? That I felt that I'd known him before, in another life? And you felt it too, didn't you Pierre? We're family! We're never going to be separated now!"

POSTSCRIPT
September 2019

In a few days' time it would be Friday, September 27th—the day that the new Mary Elmes Bridge would be opened over the River Lee in Cork. The entire Collins family would be there, as would their newly found relatives from Argelès-sur-Mer. And Emma would get to see Pierre again, her second cousin. Grandad would be there, and Mr. White, her history teacher, would be there as well. She had invited John Braddock, too, since he had played an important part in this journey.

No doubt there would be key officials in attendance and several speeches made, but Emma's friends and family would simply observe all the fuss and excitement, with the utmost pride—thankful that they were part of the many people alive today who owed their very existence to the wonderful Mary Elmes.

Of course, Emma and Pierre had been in touch over the past few weeks, there was so much to do and so much to discuss. They both knew that their futures would be in work with refugees. Emma had posted Pierre an article on suitable courses for those seeking to help refugees and asylum seekers. The only problem was that they were Masters courses and Emma and Pierre were not even undergraduates yet! There was a long way to go! Would it be a journey they could take together? What would Mary Elmes say if she were still alive now? If only they could seek her advice!

ABOUT THE AUTHOR

Bernard S. Wilson is a retired university lecturer who was born in Great Britain in 1933. He holds a BD (Hons) from the University of London and an MA in Education from the University of Leeds.

Wilson's interest in the subject of Mary Elmes and her work arises from the fact that for seven years he undertook the research that eventually led to the discovery of details showing that she saved Jewish children from deportation at the risk of her life. One of these children, Dr. Ronald Friend, then presented this information to Yad Vashem in Jerusalem which resulted in Mary's posthumous honor as "Righteous among the Nations" in 2014.

Wilson contributed to the documentary film *It Tolls for Thee* and was consulted by Clodagh Finn at every stage of the writing of her book *A Time to Risk All*. He also provided assistance to Paddy Butler in the writing of his book *The Extraordinary Story of Mary Elmes*.

Wilson is the author of the recently published children's book *Miss Mary* (2020).

To read more about *Grandad's Journey* and other stories of the Holocaust, go to: **rebrand.ly/6855fe**